# Possibilities in Parenting

# Possibilities in Parenting

Editor
Sadie Lake

Happy Publishing

POSSIBILITIES IN PARENTING

Edited and Produced by Sadie Lake

Copyright © 2015 by Happy Publishing

First Edition
ISBN:

Cover and Interior Design by Roseanna White Designs

Published by Happy Publishing, www.HappyPublishing.net

# Foreword

KATHERINE MCINTOSH

Here I am sitting at the San Diego Airport after facilitating a weekend workshop, playing on the California beaches, eating at great restaurants, meeting really cool people, exploring the city, and creating my life in a way that works for me.

I am waiting to board a plane and return home to the mountains of Colorado. It has been a week since I've seen my little monkey and I miss him. I can't wait to go home and snuggle up to him, hug him, ask him about his day, give him kisses, and watch him play. He's three years old and I can do those things with him right now. I imagine when he's fifteen, we will create a different way of interacting because snuggling with mom would be so uncool.

And right now, at three, I love being able to witness this giant-being-in-a-tiny-body navigate the journey of figuring out what it's like to be in the world and be him. He is an incredible addition to my life. He brings me so much joy and I get to play, and negotiate, and be fierce, and ask questions, and follow the rules of parenting that work for me. I also get to hold him and be the person that holds him as he negotiates his life.

When people used to ask me if I was going to have kids, my thought was always, NO WAY!

At that time, I had an amazing life and I knew if I was going to have children, it would have to be *in addition* to my life.... traveling and experiencing the world with me; parenting done different from the ways in which I had experienced it.

The examples I grew up with were parents who gave up their life and living and joy to work jobs they didn't like so their children could have a better life than them. They were stressed and unhappy. My mom always said, "In my next life, I want to come back as my children."

It wasn't exactly what I wanted to sign up for!

I was here to live NOW, not sacrifice my whole life and living so I could give my children a better life than me. What if we could both create together, a magical life?

Now that's a concept!!!

What if your children could add to your life? What if they could help co-create the magic of your life and living with you? What if having children didn't have to be a sacrifice?

Parenting is a role that no one can prepare you for....no one!

Not even the best books on parenting can allow for the change and difference in interacting with another alive, growing, changing being. Reading about how to be a parent and actually being a parent are two totally different things.

You can read about how to have the best orgasm, but having a really good orgasm requires interacting with another human being. It requires following the energy and being present in the moment with every sensation. It also requires letting go of the textbook advice and actually discovering the truth of what works for you and your body and the other person.

Parenting is a lot like that; no textbook can prepare you

for what's required when your child throws a temper tantrum, slams a door, and breaks a mirror into a million little pieces all over your living room floor, or takes a black permanent marker and draws designs all over your brand new velvet couch.

There is no textbook answer for anything about being a parent. It requires following your knowing, doing what works for you, and responding to the energies of the moment. Every parent has different expectations, thoughts, and ways that parenting works for them.

I am terrible at following the rules, so my ways of parenting have always been a bit like me: rebellious. I don't follow the rules.....and it works. It works for me to discover what actually creates the most for both my son and myself.

In the pages of this book, you will find different ways of parenting, filled with stories, questions, tools, and ways of interacting with children that are really different.

This book is an invitation to discover a new way of being and to inspire you to create a way of living with your children that would work for you. There are a million different possibilities and what if you could create your own rule book for the type of parent you'd like to be?

At the end of the day, this is your journey...

Are you up for the challenge?

Katherine McIntosh

# Table of Contents

# Chapter I

## The Joy of Being a "Bad Mother"

### By Jennifer Chabot

Before I became a mom I had a lot of ideas and fantasies about how I was going to raise my children. I truly desired to be a "good mother," no matter what it took. That ended up looking nothing like what I had expected. Although at first I had a profound ease and joy in parenting, slowly that all started to fall apart. I found that the deeper I stepped into the role of being a mom, the more I slipped away from being myself. I began to feel trapped, choice-less, frustrated, miserable and angry. In a moment of clarity and brilliant words from Glenna Rice, a facilitator of Access Consciousness®, I realized that I had to be willing to be a "bad mother" in order to be truly happy. All of the definitions, conclusions and judgments I had about what it meant to be a good or bad mother were trapping me in a no-choice universe of despair and obligation.

I started to question everything I had decided was right and wrong, good and bad, about being a mother, a father, a parent and a partner. I began a journey towards uncovering and discovering the way I was functioning unconsciously, what I was creating, and what did and didn't work for me and my family. I slowly started to reclaim, acknowledge and recreate my parenting reality. While you read this, please don't make anything I choose right or wrong, it's just a choice that works for me. We are all as unique as snowflakes. What works and what's true for me and my family may not necessarily be true for you. One of the tools in Access Consciousness is sensing what's heavy and light in your awareness to determine whether something is true for you. If something feels light, warm, yummy, expansive, then it's true for you. If something feels heavy, mucky, dirty or contractive, then either it's not true for you or there could be a lie that you have bought as being true. My hope is that my journey might be an invitation for you to become aware of *your own* parenting reality?

When I first began to explore what I would like to create as *my* parenting reality, the first awareness that I got was that I had the point of view that my child was a burden. Wow! How much of that was I projecting on my child and how much of her behavior was a reaction to my point of view? I brought this up to another facilitator, Anne Maxwell, during my first Access Bars® class and she asked me a question: "If kids weren't a burden, what would they be?" I got the awareness that my daughter could be a gift and a contribution, if only I would allow her to be. I wondered how many more expectations and projections I had about my child that created our reality together? I really had to start being honest with myself, and be willing to look at the places and spaces that I didn't desire to look or acknowledge. But I truly desired to choose something different for myself and my child so I asked more questions to unlock all of the things I had hidden from myself. "Who does this belong to? Is this mine? Or is it a point of view that I took on from everyone around me?" When I realized something wasn't my actual opinion, I could chose to obliterate it from my universe. The more I was willing to let go of other people's beliefs, the more Annabelle showed up as a gift and a contribution. Also, as an added awesome side effect, I started to perceive and acknowledge more and more the gift and contribution that *I* was. It's so funny how much even the things that we're thinking, whether it be cognitive or non-cognitive, can truly influence how our children are acting and reacting and how we perceive ourselves. What if our children are far more psychic and aware than we have been willing to acknowledge?

I became curious how this idea of being willing to be judged as a bad mother could possibly make me happier. In order to create any kind of change, I had to explore what being a good mother meant to me. I realized that somewhere I had bought the idea that a "good mother" puts everyone else's needs above her own. Does that feel light to you? That definitely doesn't work for me. I do not desire to create a reality where my needs and desires are not considered. The funny thing is that as mothers we are perceived and judged as being bad and insane when we choose something that doesn't match anyone else's needs. If we never take the time to do the things that bring us joy and pleasure, the whole family suffers. So making our needs a priority actually benefits everyone. Something Dr. Dain Heer, co-founder of Access Consciousness, suggests is taking 30 minutes each day and one whole day every week to do something that's nurturing for you and your body. How much time and space do you require to maintain your sanity? How many of the definitions, conclusions, decisions and judgments about what it means to be a "good parent" are lies?

How many of them are you using against you?

What does your child know that you're pretending not to know, or denying that you know, that if you acknowledged that you knew it, would change everything? I'm judged as a bad, irresponsible mother if I allow my children to have choice. Parents assume they always know what's best for their children, better than their children know for themselves, and that children must do as we say because we said so. Does that feel light to you? Or is it a lie? What if your children actually know what's best for themselves and their bodies? What if they know better than anyone else, including their parents? Before I became a mother I had the point of view that my children should eat what I put on the table. My first daughter Annabelle quickly pushed me to let go of that point of view. She has never eaten bread, eggs, cooked vegetables or meat (besides cured meats like salami and ham, rarely). I even tried to trick her by cutting them up into tiny pieces and putting them into dishes she really did like. She would get the spoon near her lips, and before even putting it in her mouth she would put down the spoon and push the bowl away. It was as if just by bringing it near gave her the awareness of whether or not her body desired it. And what if you know what's best for you and your body, too? How many times have you been told that you don't know what's best or what's true for you? You don't know better than your parents, teachers, doctor, uncle, aunt, brother, sister, grandma, grandpa. Does that feel light to you? Didn't you always know that you knew? Didn't it frustrate the hell out of you to never be acknowledged for what you knew? What if one of the greatest gifts that you can give your children is the freedom, the space and choice to know what they know to be true, and to acknowledge them for it?

Annabelle and I drive people crazy all the time, including her father, with the things I've allowed her to climb and jump off of, in stores, at the park, everywhere. I know that she has a brilliant awareness of what she is capable of and I am confident in her ability to do the things that she does. I vividly remember times as a child that my mom would freak out when I climbed a tree, or the house. I always knew that I wasn't in danger and that I was fully capable of getting up and down without injuring myself.

I chose to encourage Annabelle's natural, amazing dexterity and total absence of fear, rather than doubt her. Her willingness to do and try everything is so admirable, why would I desire to squash it? By nine months she started climbing, at ten months walking, and after that she was unstoppable. When I see other parents in the park, I realize and acknowledge the gift that I have been to her. I've seen other parents tell their children, "No, you can't climb that, it's too dangerous." I wonder how much cause-and-effect we create in our children's world every single day with our worries and points of view about their inability to be trusted to know their own limits. If anyone gets told enough times that they are not capable of doing something they will start to believe it. How much are we debilitating our children when we decide that we need to protect them and keep them safe? Whenever Annabelle would approach something that I knew would be challenging, I would just assist her while doing it or stand near. And once I knew she had it mastered, I wouldn't hover around her to make sure she didn't fall. I encouraged her to trust herself and her ability without imposing a limitation on her. Would some people perceive that as me being neglectful and careless? Hell yeah!! Do I care? Hell no!! Whenever she does require my help, she asks for it. What if empowering your child to trust themselves, their capacities, and their knowing is one of the greatest gifts you can give them? I'm not always calm, cool and collected when she does some of the crazy things that she does. But I continue to relax, let go, release, and destroy and uncreate anything that allows that reaction to exist. What gifts, talents, capacities and abilities does my child have and how can I nurture and encourage them?

I have had some very dark days of shame, frustration, tears, swearing and yelling. My daughter Annabelle has strength of will that is beyond compare. I vividly remember the first time she said, "No!" to me in public and ran away from me when I was insisting, "Come here right now." I immediately felt shame, went into judgment of myself and was screaming inside. It seemed that the more I insisted and the angrier I got, the stronger she persisted and reacted. A good mother or father would put the child "in their place," "show them who's boss," and demand and command that they obey. This isn't what I desired to create, so I asked a couple questions. "What would it take for me to have more ease with this? How can I be in allowance of my child saying no to me in public?"

A couple things showed up to give me the awareness I was seeking. First was a tele-call with Anne Maxwell. She asked, "What if you don't have to be responsible for the choices that your children make?" Wow! Even though I cannot control my child, I don't have to feel shame, guilt or judgment for how she acts. Next was an article which talked about how the qualities we may perceive as being difficult in children can be a gift for them as adults. We would like our children to be obedient, compliant and submissive; to do what they're told without questioning it. Yet as adults we desire for them to be leaders, assured, confident, strong-willed and independent. I would like my child to be able to say "no" to her friends, family, teachers and boyfriends in the future. With that awareness, when Annabelle yells at me in public, now I choose to smile with pride acknowledging her self-will.

As a child, if you don't do what is expected of you, how they expect you to behave and act, you are automatically labelled as a bad child and made wrong. I realized that as parent I was unconsciously doing the same thing, automatically falling into line or resisting what was expected of me. It's hard to take care of two toddlers. I quickly created a hell on earth. A stay-at-home mom cooks dinner and does the dishes every day. I actually love baking and cooking, but when I was doing them from a sense of obligation, these things became joyless, frustrating and took me forever. When I let go of my resistance, I reclaimed my love of cooking and started to sing and dance while cleaning and even got it done with speed and ease.

What is your child trying to make you aware of that you're not acknowledging? One of the hardest pills for me to swallow was the fact that most of the things that my children, or stepchildren, were doing that really angered, irritated or frustrated me, were actually things that I did myself. Shannon O'Hara, another Access Consciousness facilitator, said once in a forum that demanding that your children be conscious is fighting a losing battle if you're not willing to choose it yourself. Anytime you are trying to force or control your children to do and be something that you aren't willing to do and be yourself, you are starting a losing war. What if you don't have to view yourself as being superior or an authority over your child? What if you can learn and gain just as much from them as they can learn and gain from you? There was something that Dr. Dain Heer said in one of his classes that I loved: "What if instead, you could be their facilitator?" How could that change your relationship?

As a facilitator you remain neutral, you are not a subject matter expert, you simply be the guide and support, for them to discover what is true and what works for them. When you have a strong point of view about what your child should choose you are essentially giving them one of two choices; to align, agree and do it, or resist, react and do the opposite. My daughter tends to resist it with every fiber of her being. What if we as parents don't have to have all of the answers? What if we can actually receive contributions from our children and what they know? Instead of demanding and commanding, what if we empowered them, gave them information, and asked them questions rather than always trying to make their choices for them? This gives them the freedom to gain the awareness of what their choice will create. Do you desire for your children to make empowered decisions throughout their whole life, based on their own awareness of what their choices will create? Or would you like them to make choices based on fear, guilt, blame, shame and regret?

What have you made so vital about your role or place in society that keeps you from creating an ease, joy and elegance in parenting, beyond what you've ever imagined was possible? How true is it that any role, definition or label that we have been given, or that we have given ourselves, limits our choices and possibilities? What if you can let go of everything you've decided a good mother or father should do and have the freedom to truly be yourself? I wonder what possibilities you could create in your life with the willingness to be perceived as being bad? What if, by choosing to discover and create from what is true for you, you also inspire others to do the same? In the face of other people's judgments, projections and expectations, when I feel myself contracting or making myself wrong, although it's not always easy, I breathe, relax, lower my barriers, walls and resistance, and allow it to pass through me. This opening allows me the clarity to know what's true for me beyond my resistance and to create a greater possibility for me and my family now and in the future.

I'm choosing to be me and to do what works for me and my family. I'm willing to be the "bad mother" that many may judge me to be, and enjoy all the decadent freedom and joy that it gives me! Would you like to join me?

# About the Author

JENNIFER CHABOT

Jennifer Chabot is an Access Consciousness® Bars and Body Process Facilitator, the founder of The Elegance of Parenting, and the creator of Unleash You.

Jennifer was a brown-eyed girl, the only brunette of four beautiful sisters. She was born and raised in Calgary, Alberta by her parents who worked hard to provide for their children. They never went without clothes or food but definitely didn't live a life of luxury. The greatest gift that her parents gave her was the freedom and space to be herself. They empowered her to feel safe all alone and to make her own choices. Her mother was an open, fun-loving, joyful soul with a generosity of spirit unmatched. Her brilliant father always fostered in his children awareness beyond the five senses and always acknowledged them for their knowing.

As a child with her cheerful eyes and free spirit she could always light up a room. This little miss sunshine was always laughing, running, smiling and having fun; squeezing every last ounce of pleasure out of every moment. She was an energizer bunny of magnitude with a joy for life and living that was beyond ordinary. Jennifer was also very daring and impulsive, earning the nickname Kamikaze; she was always pushing the limits of what was possible and driving her mother crazy with all of the stunts she pulled. Climbing trees to insane heights, jumping off roofs, balancing along edges high up in the air, there was no dare or challenge that she wasn't willing to take, no limits she wasn't willing to break; no fear, just thrill and excitement.

Growing up she had a strong, independent personality with an immense caring for everyone. She never allowed others to be ridiculed or put down around her, always sticking up for those who were being bullied. Jennifer attended a small Catholic francophone school, with a small town feel. Although raised Catholic, she always perceived a possibility beyond the limitations and control of religion. She was a very bright student who always excelled with minimal effort. As a student, as soon as the teacher had finished their lessons she was always approached by other children to explain what they had missed. She seemed to have a knack for relating things to people in a way they could understand it, a way of tapping into how others functioned in order to facilitate them into greater knowing and awareness.

As a teenager, she attended St-Francis, a huge school full of hundreds of kids. Due to her strong sensitivity and awareness, attending this school was one of the most intense experiences she ever had. On the first day of school she almost puked with the magnitude of thoughts, feelings and emotions that seemed to flood her being. She started to use drugs to cope, to feel more at ease in her own skin. Although at first, she had used them to gain more of a sense of herself, eventually it consumed her. She regressed in awareness and joy and started to embody a pretend version of everything; a pretend version of herself. She rejected and alienated dear friends in exchange for her growing ego and paranoia. Drugs pushed her to stop doing and eventually forgetting all of the things that she and her body truly loved to do. Instead, she valued and made significant all of her drug experiences. Bit by bit she lost Jennifer until she no longer recognized the being standing in front of the mirror. Finally, she decided something had to change. She stopped doing hard drugs and drinking daily and started a journey towards reclaiming herself and her life. She started to emerge from her deep dark hole, but the addiction hadn't completely subsided.

The pivotal moment in Jennifer's life was the moment she found out she was pregnant. She lost her first child to a miscarriage, which, although it was agonizing in the moment, gave her one of the greatest gifts. As soon as she found out, she quit everything, but during that first month she indulged in several toxins. Just the thought that cocaine or liquor could have contributed to the loss finally solidified her resolve to quit for good. What if you don't have to use pain as a source for change?

Throughout her pregnancy, which was an incredibly joyful amazing experience for her, she began seeking something greater, something different; a way to be in the world and parenting in a way she hadn't seen before. Jennifer began to listen to several tele-seminars such as "You Wealth Revolution," "Healing with the Masters," and "Illusion to Illumination." She heard several calls from amazing brilliant masters and mentors with whom she began to recall a lot of the things that she had forgotten. She began to reclaim and expand her knowing and depth of presence. Eventually she came across something called Access Consciousness, a modality which empowers you to gain a greater awareness of yourself and the way you function in the world, using question as a tool to open up a world of possibilities. From there she dove in head first. It ignited in her the magic and flow of life that she once knew, simply making a request of the universe and having it show up with ease, breaking free of the chains binding her to fear, blame, shame, regret, guilt and obligation, and obliterating all of the spaces and places of limitation in her life. She began to regain a communion and relationship with herself, her body and others. Her life keeps getting greater everyday and her journey continues...

Jennifer is a bubbly, playful and adventurous soul always inviting people to greater possibilities. With her calming, loving presence, she has a way to bring ease, harmony and joy, effortlessly. She flows from a fresh and enthusiastic awareness, with sage-like roots beyond her years, energetically plugged-in with a depth and knowing beyond this reality.

She is a passionate and vibrant spirit that is dancing along her winding path through the forests of creation.

For more information or to contact Jennifer you can go to her website https://jenmchabot.wix.com/unleash

# Chapter 2

## Better Than What Could Have Been

BY SADIE LAKE

I wasn't one of those little girls who dreamed of her wedding. I didn't want kids. In fact, I didn't even like them. Once when I was thirteen, my mom volunteered me to babysit for some neighbor kids. Let's just say, she never did that again. I was career-bound. I was going to be important. When my teacher/educator soon-to-be-in-laws ran into my high school principal and told him their son was going to marry me, he said, "That girl is going to conquer the world."

And he was right. I just got detoured first on a 10-year trudge through the doldrums of stay-at-home-mom land. You see, I made the glorious mistake of falling in love with an amazing man who also happened to be a humanoid of magnitude. By that, I mean that he is a nurturer. He was the one who dreamed of a family; a cozy home with the pitter patter of tiny feet and a wife he could call his best friend. He built the nest, and when I landed in it, I forgot I could fly.

He painted a pretty picture of a life I had never even dreamed of, and when I found out I was pregnant just after our first anniversary, I jumped in with both feet. Perhaps it was my rebellious nature, but if I was going to create someone else's dream come true, at least I was going to do it my way. I birthed our daughter with the assistance of a midwife in a birthing pool the kitchen of our starter home in the slummy area of my hometown known as "Felony Flats," with no idea what the hell I was doing. I just knew I had to do it *right*. If I wasn't going to be important, at least I could be right.

I joined the crunchy, attachment-parenting-home-birthing-co-sleeping-non-vaccinating-extended-nursing-child-lead-weaning-make-your-own-cleaning-supplies club. I'd love to say it was like a support club, but who are we kidding? It was the club of massive righteous indignation and superiority. In other words, it was the mothering judgment club. And I was a card-carrying member.

It wasn't all bad though. My righteous points of view about what children need did allow me to create a very intimate bond with my daughter. Unfortunately, my need to be needed completely excluded my dear hubby from the love affair I was having with my baby. I'm still in awe of the fact that he was willing to take a periphery position in our lives because he could see that being everything to our child was so vital to me at the time. He's just that kind of guy.

When baby girl number two came along three years later, I was finally willing to "let" my husband begin to parent our children. He began to "help" with the girls and around the house, and I began to resent his insecure tentativeness a little less. I had this self-righteous, superior bitch thing down to a T. I had completely laid down my life for my children, cut off parts and pieces, metaphorical arms and legs, until I was a bitter nub of a woman, a useless servant with no semblance of self left to stand on. And I was disrespectful enough to conclude that it was my husband's fault.

I would love to think I am the only woman who has ever chosen this plot line in the story of her life. For the love of men, I would. But, now more than a decade later and nearly half of the founding mothers of my original judgment club seeking separation or divorce, I'm afraid this scenario may even be more common than not.

It would have been really easy to take the easy road, to choose divorce from my man. Heck! I had already divorced from myself! But again, I have never been a good follower. And my man would never have let me throw him or his dreams away just because I was being an asshole.

But in this day and age, with so much information and not enough intuition, how many of us as parents are drowning in the sea of judgment, grasping for something we can do right, and gasping for a breath of fresh air? We're so willing to trade our knowing for approval. What's the value in choosing this insanity? Our parents didn't lay in bed with us until we fell asleep, or worry if our crackers had wheat in them. We walked to school in 12 feet of snow, up hill, both directions. Our parents weren't worried about being perfect parents. In fact, for most people I know, their parents weren't even very concerned about being *good* parents. I was one of the lucky ones. I had a mom who saw me as an infinite being and always tried her best. But trying one's best with a newborn at 19 while working a swing shift at Denny's left a lot of room for *not* A+ moments. Yeah, my mom was young, single, and poor. How many people's parents didn't even have that going for them? And what does that set us up for as we begin to grow our own families? For me, it left a burning desire to do it better... to do it perfect.

Perfect as defined by whom? Everyone, I guess, which only gave more gusto to the tornado of self-judgment I was swept up in. You see, the interesting thing about being perfect is that it's a very lonely place to dwell. In fact, the pedestal is such a narrow pinpoint that no one can ever stand on it without impaling themselves. I know, because I have slain myself on the razor-sharp pedestal of perfection. And it hurt. But lucky for me, I had a husband and a couple of really cute little girls to love me and care for me and smother me in the salve of caring every time I slaughtered myself with judgment. And lucky for me, or should I say "serendipitously" for me, I found a body of personal growth work that has empowered me to see all the places I was incarcerating myself in a prison of judgment, and has held the space for me to sew back on those metaphorical severed limbs with an ever-expanding needle-sharp awareness and a shit-ton of allowance.

I would love to say that I cared enough about myself to pull up my big girl panties and demand that I create my life differently, but that would be a lie. Remember, at the time I found Access Consciousness®, I was that nub of a woman I mentioned earlier. I was down to but a stump, a shadow of my former self... a monster I no longer recognized. I would love to say I changed for me, but I was not even in the computation of the equation of my life. I knew something had to change for my girls.

A good friend of mine once said to me, when I was complaining about my daughter's strong will: "Well Sadie, do you want her to be a weak-willed child?" Her words continued to press on my tender places years later when I was playing pathetic and being a martyr. "Well Sadie, do you want your daughters to be weak-willed women?" That's what *I* had become. That's the role model *I* was being for them. How ironic that I had been such a strong woman up until I got married, and wanted my daughters to know they could go out and conquer the world if that's what they wanted, but I was dying a slow painful death, withering away, severed from the real me and suffocating from the disconnection.

I didn't even know who I was anymore. It's kind of hard to be a strong woman, wife, and mother when you aren't even connected to your own life force. I had separated from me and what I knew in hopes that being right would give me something greater. It didn't. I had become the epitome of pathetic and co-dependent. I wouldn't let my husband handle any stressful situations with our girls, but would then be overwhelmed and resentful when they sucked the life out of me and needed me for everything while he was powerless to comfort them. I used to be jealous and bitter went he out with friends or had any semblance of a social life. He would tell me "Babe, just plan something and go do it!" and I would retort pitifully, "I don't even know what I would go do!" Not a lot of trailblazing happening when you're a pathetic pile of poo, weak from self-bludgeoning, bleeding to death under the chain mail of self-imposed perfection.

I had invested so much energy into my destruction that I never even thought to ask what the creation of *my* reality might be like. I had become hell-bent on constructing a platform from which to hang myself, convinced that I was at the effect of my family, that they were too overwhelming, too needy, too loud, too whatever. It doesn't matter, you get the point. I had made them the excuse for my unhappiness, when what was really festering underneath was the poisonous point of view that I didn't have choice in how I created my life. I was unwilling to choose something different, completely vested in proving that I couldn't handle being a mom, a wife, or a homemaker. I had become the star in my own trauma drama.

If I could prove how bad it was, maybe my husband would choose for me and set me free to do what I truly wanted to do (even though I didn't even know what that might be). The ironic thing was, he was never the one who told me I couldn't. And that, my dear friends, is how you strangle yourself. I had created my life as an eternal avalanche of overwhelm. My hubby, God bless him, just kept digging me out. He'd come home from work every night to find me in a tizzy about the kids and the responsibilities of home. He wanted to help so bad but didn't really know what to do to make me happy. So he would do the next best thing: hand me a beer and send me off to recover by myself while he took over, cooked dinner, bathed, soothed, and parented our children while I sat twitching in another room. Finally, the guilt of what I was doing to my family became too much to bear and I hit a wall.

When I slammed into what felt like the end, the jolt was so powerful that it shook me out of my stupidity and I looked around and realized that I had created all of it. And I could un-create all of it. I became aware that my internal dialog of "I hate this. They have no respect for me. They just leave their shit laying everywhere because they think I'm a maid and I'll just pick it up" was actually not true. I was the center of their lives, the matriarch, and they all adore me beyond belief. And I was acting like a sniveling little brat. What I hadn't been willing or able to acknowledge was that my point of view was actually the source of all the anger, rage, fury, hate, blame, shame, regret, and guilt... all just a hamster wheel of distraction from what was staring me right in the face: I wasn't choosing to create my life in a way that worked *for* me. I had created it *against* me.

I quickly realized that the first step to ever having a life that worked for me was to stop making myself wrong for everything I had created that didn't. Beyond *what* I had chosen, was the simple awareness *that* I had chosen it. What if didn't have to be wrong for any of it? What if choices just give us more awareness? The awareness my choices gave me was that I am a powerful creator! And what else can I create now?

I can only imagine how difficult it must have been for my girls to always walk on egg shells around me, uneasy and timid, never knowing if I was going to hug them or shout at them. All they really wanted was to make me happy, but I had never been willing to let them contribute to me. When I finally dropped my barriers to receiving them, I realized that they wanted to gift their love to me more than anything in the world. What could be different if I were willing to receive it? What if I wasn't the sole source for them? What if they are co-creating this life *with* me? I had bought the insane point of view that in order to have me, I had to separate from them. What if everything is actually the opposite of what it appears to be?

Now we all laugh about how cranky and uptight I used to be. We've swept away those egg shells and now everyone has their feet on stronger foundation, one that's safe and allowing. And when I get into one of my moods, which do pop up from time to time, they have the confidence that I will receive them when they say, "You don't need to get all worked up about it"... because I don't. They can have that trust in me because I'm willing to not make myself wrong, and therefore there's nothing for me to defend against when they let me know I'm being a jerk. I'm willing to receive their contribution and allow them to show up as the gift and presence they truly BE. What if creating my life and having it be fun and ease actually required that I include my girls, my husband, and even the contribution of every molecule in the universe in the computation, as the kingdom of WE?

My whole life, I knew I had something to contribute to this

planet and everyone and everything on it. It never shows up the way you think it's going to. The catalyst for me stepping into more of my greatness was actually being willing to receive *me* in the place I was least likely look: right in the middle of a life I had concluded I never wanted. Once I was willing to give up defending that story, I was able to see that maybe what I had created was even greater than what *could* have been. What if conquering the world, eradicating limitation, and being the source for the creation of a totally different reality begins with leaping off the pedestal of perfection into the great unknown of possibility and being steadfast in our commitment to not judge ourselves or anyone else, while also acknowledging that every point of view we have and every choice we make, creates. What catalyst can my story be that may invite you to step beyond your self-imposed limitations and create a life better than you've ever dreamed of, too?

# About the Author

SADIE LAKE

Sadie Lake is a…bit of a rebel. She's not a huge fan of saying what she "is" in a biography. She is not a big fan of creating those kinds of boxes to define or contain her. The most appropriate way to describe her is to say that she is an infinite being playing a game at Earth School.

However, some of the other roles she plays include being Mom to three little girls, Wife to an amazing man, and facilitator, educator, and catalyst for the creation of a greater future here on this planet. Access Consciousness® is her modality of choice, whose tools and classes have been the sling shot that has catapulted her into greater… greater potency, greater BEING, greater presence, greater happiness, greater everything really.

One of the things that makes her different is that she's a lot like you. Say what?! She has stumbled through most of her life searching for her "purpose" with a longing and a knowing that she's here to create a different possibility… all the while judging that she was doing a shitty job that was never enough.

She has always known something greater was possible than what we've been handed by this reality. She certainly wouldn't say she's perfect at the game of life, but she would definitely say she's a winner... if for nothing else, because she has learned how to cheat the system and play outside the rules that say judgment and the polarity of right/wrong are basis of reality. She is committed to consciousness, making the demand of herself that she create beyond all her perceived limitations and be the invitation to others to choose more for themselves as well.

One of the ways she does this is by hosting a weekly internet-based radio show on A2zen.fm called *Imperfect Brilliance*, a show dedicated to uncovering what's right about you underneath all the crap you believe isn't. *Imperfect Brilliance* is also available on iTunes Podcast or at www. imperfectbrilliance.com

Sadie is also the editor, producer, and co-author of this book's predecessor, the #1 Amazon Bestseller, *Creations: Conscious Fertility and Conception, Pregnancy and Birth.*

In between feeding children, folding laundry, and mowing the lawn, she facilitates private sessions in person and via Skype, and Access Consciousness Bars®, Body Process and Core classes all over the place. She is always looking for an invitation to get out of dodge, so if you'd like some of what she's having, her motto is, "Have consciousness, will travel." You can reach her through her Facebook page, Sadie Lake ~Facilitator, Educator, Catalyst~ or http://sadielake. accessconsciousness.com.

# Chapter 3

## The Dictator's Mom

By Jennifer Cramer Windsor

I had been ready to be a mother for years when my former husband and I decided that it was finally time to add a baby to our family. To say my biological clock was ticking would be putting it mildly. It had been going off like Big Ben for at least five years.

I was so excited about having a baby and getting the nursery ready. I bought all the books I needed to read to become an expert mother; books like *What to Expect When You are Expecting* and *The Baby Whisperer*. I devoured them cover-to-cover and back again in preparation for our child to come into the world and for me to be prepared for this new phase in our lives.

When I developed gestational diabetes, I did everything I was supposed to. I changed my diet to restrict carbs and took insulin and checked my blood sugar regularly. I was so careful that I had to start taking my blood test from my toes because my fingers were raw from pricking them. Despite my best efforts at staying healthy, I had terrible nausea, heartburn and was exhausted for most of my pregnancy.

When Griffin was ready to be born, he took such a long time to come out that the doctors decided I needed a caesarian section. He was a plump eight-pound, half ounce baby boy and was sweet and gentle... for exactly 90 minutes.

In an instant, I became a nervous mother of a very loud and demanding baby boy. I read all the books and consulted all the experts trying to figure out what to do with this baby. Nothing seemed to work for him for more than a few days, other than carrying him around constantly while he fussed.

I started to have nightmares where I would forget to feed him, or I would lose him in my house or forget him in a store. The exhaustion from having to care for this constantly-crying baby was crippling. I went to my doctor and was prescribed medication for Postnatal Depression or "Baby Blues." All it did was make me slightly less anxious and a lot more tired.

When Griffin was eight months old he managed to figure out how to climb out of his crib and get to the door of his room and sneak out. When he was ten months old, he was able to get the door knob protector off and escape out of his room quietly enough to get into other parts of the house. At just over a year, he managed to take his push-car-with-the-roof over to the fence, climb up the car and boost himself over the fence and out of the yard... and he was lightening fast.

By this time I now had two babies to care for as our second son, Raleigh, was born when Griffin was eleven months and fourteen days old. As soon as I would sit down to nurse the baby, Griffin would instantly be up to some mischief.

I lost whatever sense of self I had left during those days. My relationship with the boys's father had become increasingly difficult and so we separated when the boys were only three and two.

Griffin, already a manipulative genius at age three, would tell me giant fibs like, "Daddy wants you to move back in with him," and would also grill me about why Daddy and I broke up and ask why I didn't "still want to live in the blue house."

I bought every parenting book that promised a solution for how to get along with this demanding little dictator. I tried using the "naughty chair," putting him in his room, taking away toys, a point system for good deeds… you name it, I tried it. I even instituted a "Baby Boot Camp." Since he wanted to be such a little man, I explained to him that he would get one chance to listen and if he didn't then he would get one spank on a bare bottom. If he didn't listen again he would get two spanks, etc. This worked for a day or so until he decided that a few spanks wasn't going to stop him from getting what he wanted and that Mom wasn't nearly as tough as she tried to be.

During this time I was offered a job in Vancouver working for a bank. I made somewhat amicable arrangements to move the children with me to a quaint little suburb called Burnaby. My family was all living in Vancouver so I was relieved to move away from the town were the boys were born, to get away from the usual post-divorce snubs from all the still-married Stepford Wives. Instead of having a husband, I hired a live-in nanny. I was of the opinion that the boys should be able to play with friends at their own house and that they should be able to be at home. Although it was a much more expensive option, it was worth it at the time.

Griffin had a not-so-great time in Kindergarten. A little dictator does not listen to teachers or teachers' assistants; a principal maybe… from time to time. He was also attracted to more dominant style friends who later "turned coat" and tattled on him when it was discovered what mischief that they had been up to. My son, the little dictator with no mind for political intrigue.

Griffin had even less fun in Grade One. There were two teachers in the class and they were polar opposites. One was smart enough to get the little dictator on her side, the other tried to be the bigger dictator. This did not fly with Griffin. There were incidents after incidents at school, so much that I began taking him to a homeopath to see if we could ease his school days with something natural rather than going the Ritalin route that so many other parents were choosing. I also was not excited about having him tested or diagnosed with any particular "illness." I was, and still am, of the opinion that once a child is diagnosed all it does is point a finger in one direction for the rest of their lives.

I started to set aside a special time in the evenings, after Raleigh would go to sleep, when Griffin and I would lay on the couch and listen to Anthony Robbins together. No talking, just listening. I remember Griffin, at six years old, saying to me, "Mom, this guy is really smart." I treasured these few quiet, conflict-free moments with my son, knowing that we both required something that we didn't have a clue how to get from each other.

His terrible time at school, coupled with wonderful visits to his Dad's house where they went on boats and bought presents, got Griffin thinking. He started telling his father fibs, like that I locked him outside, that I locked him in his room, and that I left him to babysit his brother. He was telling me fibs too, but I was aware of what a little truth-bender he was and it mostly made me laugh.

The lies caught up to me when I received a summons to court. My ex-husband was seeking an ex parte order for custody of the children on the grounds of child abuse. I went to court with all the documents together including six affidavits signed by various people in the boys's life, including the homeopath and a neighbor I barely knew except that our kids played together. Despite my best preparation, the judge ruled that the children would have primary residence with their father.

During the next five years, I spent tens of thousands of dollars fighting the Court's decision. I felt like everything that I ever wanted to be or do with my life was taken away in one afternoon. Every decision that I had made, every incident with the children scrutinized daily by both myself and by the children's new Stepmother, until I really did want to die. To say she was cruel would be putting it mildly. She would threaten to not let me see the kids every time I had visitation. She would listen in on their phone calls with me and correct me or the children if she didn't like what they were asking or what I was saying. She called herself their mother and made every attempt to erase me from their lives so that they didn't really know who I was.

I had become so depressed I was planning on leaving the planet. I probably would have except that I wasn't quite sure how I could do that with the least impact on those that I loved.

It was during this time that I happened to be listening to an internet radio show and came across Access Consciousness®. The facilitator was talking about how 98 percent of our thoughts and feelings are not even ours and this resonated so strongly with me. I was always having people say to me, "Oh, thanks for calling me, I was just thinking of you!" or, "How did you know I was hurting there? You know just what to do with your hands to take my pain away."

One of the things that was recommended on the radio show was to have my "Bars" run. Later I learned that the Bars® is a body process in Access Consciousness for changing what seems unchangeable. I went for a session and things did start to change for me, so slowly and regularly that my life was really never the same. At work, I was offered more money and more opportunity with better clients. At home, I was getting smarter with my money and pulled it together to get a roommate. In my personal life, I was using the tools of Access and attracted a lovely Soulmate partner.

I was curious and wanted more information about Access Consciousness so I took a Bars class with a local facilitator and then took Foundation and Level One a short while later.

During the Foundation and Level One class, I learned some tools that later allowed me to create a much better relationship with Griffin.

I had started to run his Bars when I saw him, at least once a visit. This allowed him to make some changes in his life, too, one of which was to examine the medicine that his doctor put him on and see that it was an anti-psychotic that could damage his heart if he took it for more than a short time. He told his father that he was going to stop taking the medicine and he and I weaned him off over the summer break. There were still a few yelling matches, tantrums and threats that summer but it was less than any previous visit we had ever had before.

At this point, I had taken Level 2 and Level 3 with Access Consciousness where I learned to choose what kind of relationship I was going to have with my son and how to create it. I also learned to destroy and uncreate everything our relationship was yesterday and any expectations of what it will be today. This allowed us to begin to create our relationship anew instead of functioning from old default patterns or worrying about what happened yesterday.

Gary Douglas, the founder of Access Consciousness, challenged me to have a "who cares" attitude about parenting. If my children were going to call me a bitch anyway, who cares what I do? I learned to ask, "How much fun can I have today being the pathetic pile of crap parent I truly be?" That way I am asking for fun while also being willing to be a pathetic parent. It's amazing what fun it can be messing with my kids' expectations of me. By *being willing* to be a pathetic parent, I was able to stop judging all of my choices. If I didn't have to try to be perfect, then I could just be me and have fun with my kids. What a difference this made for us! Now when I feel judgment coming on from them or from myself about my parenting, I just laugh and use my Access Consciousness tools like "Fun Pathetic Parent." It's amazing how many genuine compliments I get from them, like, "You are the BEST Mom ever!" and, "Don't worry Mom, you are the greatest!" Now I am willing to be "cute but not bright" about my parenting style, rather than rigid and by-the-book.

Griffin entered Air Cadets, a life-long ambition of his, at 12 years old. As a baby, I would make a deal with him that if he would come with me to the grocery store and not cry or act out, he could have a toy plane. He collected dozens of these replica airplanes over the years, and to this day can always tell us what model of plane it is flying overhead. Air Cadets has been everything Griffin hoped it could be.

This year he went away for three weeks to Air Cadet Camp. Instead of the getting into the Top Gun Flight Camp of his dreams, he was sent to Physical Education Camp where he learned the rules of a bunch of sports instead. He is not really a sporty kid, he prefers computers. Not having his essential alone time, coupled with his homesickness, set him up for a bit of difficulty maintaining concentration and keeping his spirits up. During this challenging time he text-messaged me asking for assistance. Instead of "poo-pooing" what I had to offer, he really listened and thought about how he could apply the Access Consciousness tools to the situation he had created for himself. If 98 percent of his thoughts and feelings were not his, then maybe the thoughts of wanting to quit and go home might not be his either. If he thought that the sergeants orders were strange or not in alignment with Camp orders, then he may be tapping into others' thoughts. I also taught him to ask, "How does it get any better than this?" and wait for signs of improvement, and to ask, "What else is possible?" to invite new possibilities to show up.

He graduated from his camp and learned everything that was asked of him. He even won an award for "Fastest Orienteering" and also gained a wealth of experience about being independent and playing with a team. He is now working on a project to get all of the flight simulators working for his local squadron and I can easily see this becoming a dynamic and fun province-wide gig.

While Griffin might always be a dictator at heart, with the tools of Access Consciousness and an inept, pathetic Mom, at least he is learning to be a benevolent one.

# About the Author

JENNIFER CRAMER WINDSOR

Jennifer came to this planet with an inner knowing of how people work and a laser-sharp ability to draw lines in between what people were saying, what they were doing and what they were actually hoping to accomplish. Jennifer started speaking at four months of age and not too long afterwards, ideas about what people could do differently would pop into her head and out her mouth they would fly!

Telling adults what they are doing wrong and what they could do to improve their lives wasn't popular; Jennifer was often in trouble for sharing her findings.

Jennifer learned to read at age three and loved using new words and reading giant books. Luckily, her Mom was excited by her thirst for knowledge and bought her new books regularly. Jennifer combed the house for anything exciting to read and found not only novels and *National Geographic* magazines, but also the dictionary, the *Bible*, *The Way* and *Colliers Encyclopedias.* Jennifer found in reading a ready friend to entertain her and nourish her famished curiosity about people.

Jennifer started attending self development courses at sixteen. When the people in her class discovered that she was not an adult, they were surprised and annoyed that she had insight beyond her years. Jennifer used to allow this to mean something about her, that she was too candid, too blunt, too helpful and that it was somehow all too much for the world around her. For many years she dialed it back, dulled it down and tried to stuff herself into the box that everyone around her seemed to fit into so stylishly.

In early adulthood, Jennifer discovered a capacity for real estate and in turn, sold, financed and managed residential, commercial and investment properties working in this field for the majority of her adult life. Jennifer used her capacities to change some of the processes for financing and managing real estate so that the people who lived there could enjoy their homes more and have the real estate gain value, so it did!

Jennifer's first discovered Access Consciousness® in 2010 while listening to an internet radio show. A facilitator was explaining how 98 percent of our thoughts and feelings are not even ours. Jennifer had a "light bulb moment" that perhaps she *wasn't* too much; she was just more aware of the thoughts and feelings of the people around her than the average person.

Jennifer was so excited about this new knowledge that she jumped right in and right away got her Access Consciousness Bars Facilitator license. Quickly thereafter, she went on to become an Access Consciousness Certified Facilitator as well as an Access Body Process Facilitator.

Helping people become more aware of what they know about their lives is Jennifer's full-time job and she couldn't be happier. Jennifer's clients laugh when things fly out of her mouth that they have been thinking or feeling for years!

Jennifer's biggest hope for her clients is that they stop looking to the past to create their future and that she can be the catalyst for them creating the life that they always knew was possible and didn't know how to initiate. Jennifer asks herself every day, "How did I get so lucky?" and is so thrilled with the changes that she has made to her everyday life with the tools of Access Consciousness.

If you have discovered a burning desire for change in your life and living, Jennifer is available worldwide for group and private coaching programs with both individuals and corporations. Jennifer loves to facilitate Access Consciousness Foundation classes, Bars and Body Classes as well as specialty classes like "Conscious Coupling." Jennifer's web site is accessholistic.com and she invites you to connect with her on Facebook at Jennifer Cramer Windsor.

# Chapter 4

## Beautifully Imperfect Parenting

### By Cassy Summers

I once believed if I could look ahead and do everything right, my kids would have the happy, emotionally perfect childhood I never had. As my oldest turns five and my youngest dances around the two-and-a-half year mark, I find myself: separated from my husband, starting my own business, rocking some strange hair, with some strange world views, and overall, quite unusual.

I may have failed the perfect part....

And yet, I see the beauty, the growth and the possibilities in this imperfection.

### ~A Child's Awareness~

In the basement, Zak and Xander are exploring as I unpack our new life out of squashed and miscellaneous boxes. I notice Xander watching me for a little while and then he asks me the question most parents would dread. "Mommy, why don't you and Daddy live together anymore?" His face held a shadow of curiosity but mostly a sense of heaviness and confusion.

I stopped unpacking and looked him in the eyes, searching for the greatest possibility. I went to question, "Xander, what do you know about Mommy and Daddy living together?"

"Not happy," he responded right away.

Then I asked, "What do you know about Mommy and Daddy living apart?"

I gave space to the question and allowed his eyes and energy to wander. Then he came back to me. His eyes lit with awareness and the heaviness lifted from his face. "Happy!" he said, smiling at me.

I smiled back as we exchanged energetic whispers of the acknowledgment of even more joy to come. I scooped up that brilliant boy and hugged him dearly. I knew this happiness to be true for me. I knew as well that this chapter of our lives would be filled with adventure, joy, gratitude and creation.

What if honoring a child's awareness could be that easy and that simple? The more I acknowledge these boys' incredible knowing, the more it grows. They continue to astound me with what they know about the world around them.

Acknowledging and exploring awareness is not about becoming a back seat driver and having your kids run you. It is more about being a true leader and supporting and contributing to those that are with you. What if we allowed our children to be leaders along with us? What if we allowed them to contribute to us?

The idea that there can only be one leader creates a sense of competition and separation. That is not communion. These people-with-small-bodies have enormous capacities to lead and change the world. For me, that is something to be nurtured, honored and acknowledged. How this shows up for you and your family will be beautifully unique. The greatest way I have found to create this is by asking questions. I ask my kids real, true questions, with curiosity and presence. I go into question for myself and wonder each day, "What will it take to out-create yesterday?"

The dance of parenting these incredible, intelligent, and aware boys is something I am constantly playing with and looking to see where I can be greater. I have given up perfectionism and instead took up dancing! It holds way more joy and growth for me as every time I label something as perfect, it has to stay exactly as it is for it can never be greater if it's already labeled perfect. I am still clearing out the museum of dusty old perfectionism. But as I move forward, the old building seems vacant and ready to be torn down.

## ~Creating Any Day to Be Phenomenal~

Groceries, laundry, commitments, and on and on... these are the things that can be daunting and quite boring for children and let's admit it, for us too. I have had days where I dragged my littles from place to place getting things done; the pressing needs around me leading the day. These are not our most joyful or expansive days.

What if you could create any day to be phenomenal no matter what you are doing?

Each morning, I create the day with my boys. They like to do this in the playroom so that their hands are occupied as we talk. I give them the information and the energy of everything I desire to do that day and then I ask them what they would like to do as well. When I speak about giving the energy of something, I am referring to when you go beyond the *doing* of the day and into how you would like it to *be*. Would you like a day full of joy, adventure, calm, quiet? Maybe all of it? You can give that energy to them as you describe your desires for the day. Sometimes when I ask the boys there is an explosion of ideas and creations, and other days it's simple and easy. Then we look at how we can create this together.

For example, if we are going to the grocery store I will ask them questions such as, "What would be fun to do in the grocery store? Play a game as we shop? Pick out your own fruit or vegetable? Take some time to look at books or magazines? Dance party in the aisle?!"

I used to think I didn't have time to dawdle in the store. This perfect mom had many tasks jammed into everyday. What I have noticed is that when I am willing to relish in the three minutes it takes Xander to explore the peppers and Zak to chat with the cute girl in the shopping cart, I have just saved ten minutes of resistance, frustration and possible meltdown somewhere else.

Growing up I was never told that I could create my life; it was explained to me that you make do with what life gives you. Doesn't that seem heavy and void of possibilities? Think of all the people that have created great change in this world... did they just make do? Or did they create a new reality?

Something I would like to gift my children is the awareness that they can create their lives, that they can create every day. This looks different with each person and the age or place they are in. So, if you desire this as well, you can begin with just asking them the question, "What would you like to create today?" They may not have an answer and if you ask yourself this question too, you may not have an answer either, and that's ok. Maybe you just have a sense of an energy of nurturing or adventure? It's not about defining it, it's about an awareness. What if you didn't look for an answer and instead you looked for the possibilities the question opens up?

For my family it has allowed a deeper communion, an exchange of energies and desires being met. The days we are creating, we function as a collective moving together to create and receive the greatest of possibilities the day has available. I wonder what magic lies in the grocery aisle for you?

## ~Intimacy With Children~

What does intimacy with your children mean to you? The word intimacy has many ideas attached to it, but what if it was actually a totally limitless way of gifting and receiving with your children?

Access Consciousness® talks about the concept of "Intimacy" as an energy that gets created from honor, trust, allowance, vulnerability, and gratitude. This is something I have chosen to commit to having with my children and with myself. What would it be like to be truly intimate with you and every member of your family?

## Honoring

My boys are both so different and desire and require different things. For me, part of honoring them is to acknowledge what works and doesn't work for each of them and not force them to twist themselves into fitting someone else's expectations, including mine.

Xander is often very kind, sweet and affectionate. He loves to sit on my lap and nuzzle in. He looks deep into my eyes and strokes my cheek. And, there are times when he doesn't like to be touched, even by me. He doesn't desire to hug a relative or even high five his friends. I do not make him wrong for this. Growing up, this would not have been an acceptable behavior. It was considered rude in my family, and I would have been expected to do these things anyway. I noticed that for me it created a sense of not owning my body, and deciding that in order to be a kind person I had to make everyone around me happy and comfortable even if it meant I was uncomfortable.

Is this truly honoring of anyone?

This may bring up things that happened in your own childhood or in your own family dynamic. If so, I invite you to not align with or defend against your own experience. What if instead you could ask a question about what is true for you regarding all of this? What would you like to create going forward?

## Trust

Trust is not blind faith. Trust is never giving up your awareness for someone else's. What if trust was more about knowing that people will always do what they have decided is best for themselves? And with that, you can trust what you know in regards to someone, without concluding that every day they will be the same. I can trust that Zak will demand to put his own shoes on when I forget and try to do it for him. I can trust that Xander will always ask me to carry his school bag, until the day comes when he suddenly asks to carry it himself. You see, it is ever-changing, especially with children as they are so willing to change. I trust that my boys will always request what they perceive is best for themselves.

This does not mean that if you have trust that you cannot still ask questions to create awareness for either you or them. An example would be when a child tells you that they are not tired and their body shows you the signs of fatigue. Trusting them does not mean that you should allow them to stay up as long as they desire, unless of course that works for you and your family. What if it was more about trusting that the child has decided that staying up would be the more fun for them, in which case you could ask them a question. "What would staying up create for you and your body? What would sleep create for you and your body?" This works better when you are in total allowance of their awareness and not impressing your parental point of view when asking these questions. I invite you to infuse curiosity in every question... because really, is it truly a question if you have already decided the answer?

For some, this may be a totally different way to look at the world. I wonder if you could have allowance for however this shows up for you and your family.

## Allowance

What is this allowance?

Well, Access Consciousness defines "allowance" as everything just being an interesting point of view. Do you perceive the space and ease that can create? If everything is just an interesting point of view, can you really judge yourself or your parenting?

Would you gift that kind of allowance to yourself right now?

Think of the last time you "messed up." Maybe you lost it, you yelled, or you forgot something important, whatever it was for you. Now say, out loud if you can, only because it's more fun that way for me, "Interesting point of view that I messed up. Interesting point of view I caused upset. Interesting point of view I said I would never do that again. Interesting point of view I did it again." Keep going until you run out of interesting points of view about the subject. Is it kinda fun? Is the whole thing less charged and lighter overall?

This is allowance. You can use this exercise with anything and anyone. What if everything that seems awful was just an interesting point of view?

## Vulnerability

For me, being vulnerable with my kids means having no barriers between us. This allows for a greater communion with them and everything going on in their worlds. It also means they are able to access my world. As parents, how often do we try to protect children from what is coming up for us? We hide it and put the walls up. What if that actually creates less communion and contribution with each other?

There is a difference between putting your upsets and problems onto your kids, and being vulnerable. During the separation with ex-husband I desired to keep them out of it, to put a protective blanket around these young boys and never have them feel wrong or bad about any of it. What I realized was that my desire to protect them actually limited what they could receive from me. These energetic barriers we use to protect ourselves or others will cut off gifting and receiving.

I do not initiate conversations with my kids about what is occurring regarding me and their Dad, but I do not put up barriers to it either. We have created a dynamic where they know they can ask me anything and rather than always giving them answers, instead, I like to ask them questions that guide them to their own awareness. This is one of the greatest gifts I can be for my boys.

## Gratitude

The gratitude I have for Xander and Zak often brings tears to my eyes. I am grateful for the way they *be* in this world and I am grateful to be a part of the lives they are creating. What would it be like if we could have gratitude for the gifts our children are even when they are driving us crazy? What would it be like if you were willing to be grateful for you and acknowledge the gift that *you* are, even during the times you are driving your kids crazy?

If you would be willing to play with this, I invite you to find a quiet place to sit and relax. Then ask all your barriers to lower. All barriers down, even if you don't have a cognitive idea what that is. Now, gratitude is an energy that you can receive. So with all these barriers lowered, you can ask to receive the energy of the gratitude your kids truly have for you. Sometimes your barriers will shoot right back up and that is ok, just request for them to lower again and begin receiving the gratitude. Maybe start with one person and then the next, going through your family. For some of you, this will be really easy and you may even have tears come to your eyes with the acknowledgement and receiving of this energy. And for some, this maybe new for you. If you desire, you can do this once a week and just notice if it gets easier or if something changes.

When I am choosing to have gratitude for my children, I have so much more ease with all the little hiccups along the way. I wonder how much more your kids are able to receive from you when you come from this space as well?

### ~Beautifully Imperfect~

What I have noticed with my clients and friends is that every family has its own symphony; a compilation of energies, personalities, experiences and targets. Some have more harmony than others. What will create that harmony, that explosion of exquisite melody, is different for each symphony. So what I would like to invite you to, most of all, is a sense of play and creation with parenting and with your family.

What if we didn't have to have all the answers? What if instead we had curious questions? And what if we were willing to see the beauty and creation in the imperfections? What brilliance and joy of parenting would truly be possible then?

What if my beautifully imperfect parenting was the gift I always knew I could be?

# About the Author

CASSY SUMMERS

Dear Curious You,

What would you like to know about me?

My past, my present, my possible futures? The wonderings of my universe? The magic of my creations? The awakening of me?

In 2012 Access Consciousness® came into my life and gave me the most phenomenal gift I have ever received... **ME**. It woke up the person I had put to **sleep**, the person I had made **wrong for being**. And now I had **tools** to have ease with all the chaos and suffering I perceived around me.

The information they were sharing and what they were speaking to was everything I had always know was **possible** but had been told was was **impossible**. I remember sitting in my first Foundation class, one of the core classes of Access Consciousness, and thinking **"I knew it!"** And the beautiful thing is, that I truly did know and I am still discovering and uncovering all that I know, all that I had labeled as impossible.

I immersed myself in the tools, the questions, and everything available through Access Consciousness. I couldn't get enough! I traveled to classes and read everything I could get my hands on. I am a little obsessive like that sometimes (insert wink here) and found myself expanding and changing at an incredible rate. The more I received, the more **ease**, **joy**, and **glory** (exuberant expression of abundance) I began creating and having.

I began to acknowledge my unique way of parenting and how different I am with people.

I began to acknowledge my gifts with facilitation and creation.

The definition I have found for "facilitate" is to **"make (an action or process) easy or easier."** This is what I do... what I have always done actually, for everyone around me. When someone is **asking for change**, I create an easier, faster **path** to get there. Stepping into this has turned me on to a more **vibrant** and **generative** way to live.

What could be greater than contributing change and consciousness to the beautiful people in this world?

Acknowledging the wonderful uniqueness of me and finally using my gifts has been like opening these **incredible wings** I had **tucked away**. How lucky am I to have these phenomenal children to contribute to, that are always so willing to receive and request more of me?!

There is much more to share and many things I would love to gift to you but I enjoy and acknowledge the **possibilities created with questions**. So I encourage, maybe even dare you, to ask me whatever questions that are rising and dancing in your world.

Always in such gratitude

Cassy Summers
Curiousuniverse.ca
curious.universe.cassy@gmail.com

# Chapter 5

## The Joy and Pragmatics of Parenting

### By Heather Nichols

For the first many years of being a mother, to be honest, I kind of hated it. I was constantly assessing myself against all of the expectations and judgments of what constitutes a "good mom." My whole life, I knew that I would eventually have two kids. I studied child development in college, got a Masters degree in Social Work, and "knew" a lot about the human psyche, about child psychology, and, frankly, about all the ways we can potentially "fuck up" our kids. After all, I was the therapist that sat with adults hashing through their childhood traumas, woundings, and all the places and spaces where they were grossly misunderstood, let down, projected upon, and molded to fit into someone else's reality.

So I knew it all. I had seen it all. And I was not going to be *that* mom who wasn't totally tapped into her kids. My plan was—be the perfect mom; the mom who understood my kids 100 percent; the mom who knew what they were feeling before they knew; the mom who would give them everything from the best home-made organic raw baby food to the non-plastic toys to the most nurturing presence to all of the experiences a child could desire and more to have a stellar, thriving childhood that they would surely rave about in their adult years. Sound fun to you? Me neither.

And then, my two colicky babies were born two and a half years apart. I was not the mom who was going to have a baby that cried all the time! Because I was going to be that mom who responded to their every need—in advance. After months and months of trying everything to get my baby to not cry (including limiting my own diet to a total of four foods)— and failing miserably—I finally realized that the fantasy I had about motherhood was just that: a total lie. The "good mom" was in fact a fantasy; a fabricated story, a distraction that moms everywhere could use to judge themselves into eternal wrongness for never getting the most judge-able job in the world "right." Add to that a divorce when my kids were one and three, and it was time to start that future therapy fund after all.

The thing was, the fantasy that I would so love every moment of my time with those precious babes just was not my reality, especially as a single mom. And nobody else seemed to feel that way. The moms around me would talk for hours on end about the perfect organic sunscreen, or that amazing recipe for getting raw greens in their picky toddlers. They would share what they had learned from the sleep books and the parenting books and the experts and the everybody-that-had-a-point-of-view-about-the-kids. After all, I live in Boulder, Colorado: The Capital of Perfect Parenting. Give your three-year-old candy before noon, or put them in front of the TV, and Child Protective Services might get involved.

## What Does The Body Have to Do With It?

My body was constantly giving me signals, information, and feedback about what worked for me as a mom. And actually, my children's bodies were too. And I was a "body person"! But somehow, even though I would guide my clients to receive all kinds of information from their bodies that would change their lives, the massive amounts of judgment I had about me just did not allow me to have clarity around what my body was telling me, showing me, and sometimes begging me to change.

I found Access Consciousness® and started to have conversations and take classes that invited me to a totally different reality of being, knowing, perceiving, and receiving as a parent. I quickly realized how much judgment was in our world and in my world around parenting and the ridiculous goal of perfection. And I realized that my body had been showing me a different possibility all along. It was time to toss out the parenting books, stop consulting the "experts," and actually acknowledge both my body—and my children—as the experts in what was going to work for my family.

I went to an Access Consciousness Body Class with the founder of Access, Gary Douglas, and I asked him about the back pain I had been having since my kids were born. He asked me a question that nobody else had had the guts or the awareness to ask me: "Do you sometimes hate being a mom?" Gulp. In a room full of 100 people, microphone in my hand, I uttered a "Yes." Then he suggested I hire a nanny so that I could do more of what I loved to do, and suggested that this might help my back pain.

My body sighed with relief at the thought of it. Two weeks later, the nanny was hired, my back pain was gone, my business started thriving, and my kids had a new "manny" in their lives who they were absolutely smitten with. He was way more fun than me. And his presence in our family made all of us happy.

This was the beginning of me really getting that my body, and my children, know exactly what they require. And that if I choose something that makes me happy as a mom, and that nurtures and honors and supports me and my body—my kids always benefit from it. Who grew up with a mother who was a martyr and is grateful that she sacrificed herself over and over for them? Giving ourselves up for our children never actually creates more for anybody—including them—and this has finally become the primary space from which I've been parenting for the past four years.

I have not had that kind of back pain again. And motherhood has become more and more fun, joyful, easeful, and delightful for me ever since.

## What Do the Kids Know?

One of the major changes I have made in "how" I parent my kids is that I recognize that they are infinite beings. They are not naive little people who don't know things about themselves. They are four trillion-year-old beings, and they have the awareness of lifetimes. The primary point of view I function from as a mom is that my children know more about themselves than anybody else does—including me. I trust their awareness. I ask them what they know. I empower them to make choices for themselves that most parents would never allow. And my body, and my awareness, always let me know if more questions need to be asked, or if more information is required.

I trust my kids. I trust their awareness. I trust my awareness. And I trust my body.

My target as a mom is no longer to be the perfect mom. My

target is to raise my children to totally trust themselves, and to know that their awareness is the most powerful thing they have in the world. My target is to nurture the spark of creative brilliance that is already so alive in each of them, so they know that they can create anything they would like to create in their lives, and *as* their lives.

So I ask them questions—all the time. They let me know in no uncertain terms if something needs to be changed, or if there is something that is not working for them. We have a trust and an ease with each other that is rare, different, and weird to some. How we live and how we be with each other may be judge-able to a lot of people who are still functioning from the point of view that parents are superior to their kids.

So many experts out there purport the points of view provided by the research and the longitudinal studies that are designed to take us out of awareness as parents and put us into the box of "not-fucking-up." Yet these studies and points of view don't account for the fact that we are all *so* different. Every one of us knows something so unique that is a contribution to the world if we allow ourselves to know what we know. There is no parenting book out there that can teach you what you need to know about your children and your family. *You* are the ones who know.

When my babies wouldn't stop crying, I tried everything. I am so grateful now that none of the "solutions" worked to change the intensity of what was occurring in my world and in their world. My kids were literally demanding that I ask questions and talk to them—even as newborn babes. And while it took me a few years to get the memo, I now see what a gift that period of time was to me. I was never going to be the mom that could figure it out. I had to trust my awareness, I had to trust my body, and I had to trust my children.

Being a Judge-able Parent

The willingness to be totally judged as a mother has been one of the greatest choices for freedom in my life. I don't cook much for my kids, or pick them up from school most of the time. I don't go to PTA meetings. I do, however, have a fabulous nanny who does a lot of that so that I can do what I love—create my business and do whatever I possibly can to inspire people to choose and have a reality that works for them. And when the boys come home, happy from their after-school adventures, I am there, available, not distracted by laundry or cooking or cleaning—and we get incredibly delicious time with each other. My children require me, my body, and the space that I be. They don't require me to do all the superfluous stuff that proves to other people that I'm a good mom.

Parenting can be one of the most challenging choices we make—so why torture ourselves by continually assessing ourselves against an ideal that doesn't work for us? Your joy is essential to your children. Are you willing to choose it, no matter what? Whatever it looks like? And it may look nothing like my joy, or anybody else's. What is it that lights you up in regards to your children and your family? What would it create if you chose that and let go of everything else that keeps you from having it?

## Allowance

Allowance is an energy that is practically non-existent in this reality. Allowance is a *space of being* that expands possibility, goes beyond judgment, and is a key element of intimacy. For me, parenting with allowance requires that my body be involved. Parenting with allowance means that I am curious about who my children are every day. Parenting with allowance means that I have a lot of space for my children to choose what is going to work for them, and that I don't have a point of view that any of their choices are "right," "correct," or, "wrong."

Parenting with allowance also means that I am honoring of me and what lights me up. It is the demand that I make of me to create my life, living, and reality pragmatically—with the recognition and trust in who I am rather than the judgment of who I should or shouldn't be.

Parenting with allowance is about being willing to be *any* energy that is required. Sometimes it's a burst of potency. Sometimes it's a manipulation to get them to choose something different that works for me. Sometimes it's about letting them fall, hurt themselves, flail, make mistakes. Sometimes it's about adoring, celebrating, and acknowledging them in ways that many people are never celebrated, honored, and adored.

Parenting with allowance is a deep honoring of the beings that my children *be*. It is also a deep honoring of who *I* be, and the choices that the three of us have made to be together, to play together, to be the sweet and potent and crazy family that we be. It is a recognition that my children chose me as their mom—and that they wouldn't have chosen me to be somebody that I am not. They chose me for me. And the more me I be, the more they get to see that they can be *them* fully as well.

How did I get so lucky to be Avery and Jaden's mom? After 10 years, I can now truly say that I love most of my moments with them, and I am beyond grateful that they chose me!

# About the Author

HEATHER NICHOLS, MSW

Heather Nichols, MSW, has been playing and creating in the field of change, magic, and transformation her whole life, and professionally since 1997. She has worked extensively with bodies as a somatic psychotherapist, movement facilitator, and hands-on healer; has created and facilitated the growth of countless businesses; has had her own business for over 20 years, and has been a single mom-preneur for a decade. Heather's point of view is that everything in our lives can be a contribution to everything else—our children, our relationships, our bodies, our businesses—and she loves to travel the globe meeting new people and inviting them to choose the inconceivable possibilities that are available to them in this dynamic time of change. Heather is an Access Consciousness® Certified Facilitator, a Joy of Business™ Certified Facilitator, a business consultant, healer, author, and international speaker.

Heather Nichols, MSW
www.heathernichols.com

# Chapter 6

## Totally Different Dad

By Brendon Watt

If I could have one target for the "Totally Different Dad" classes I teach, it would be to help parents learn to recognize themselves, and to recognize their kids for who they are rather than a projection of themselves or anyone else.

Growing up was an interesting time for me. I remember, as an eight-year-old, hiding behind a tree at school one day, crying and thinking to myself, *"I cannot remember one day in my life that I haven't cried."* I just didn't get it. *"What is this place about? Why do people treat each other the way they do? Where do I fit in?"*

I spent the next 22 years of my life trying to fit in. Have you ever felt like the round peg in the square hole? Did you look to see what someone would think of you before making a choice, as if their judgments would somehow make it ok? I know that if you are reading this book you are seeking something different. Here are some tools I have used that have given me so much more ease with parenting and have allowed me to create the life and living that work for me. I wonder if they might contribute to you, too?

At 30, I was a single dad sharing a room with my four-year-old son at my mother's house. I would wake up next to this little guy thinking, *"How the hell do I show him how to be him when I have no idea how to be me?"*

When I found out that Nash's mum was pregnant, I remember thinking, *"Finally, the solution to my problems."* I didn't realize at the time how unkind this was to him, to project and expect that my son would be the savior of my life. How would that allow him to create his life? Or would he have to fight for mine? I had made my son my primary relationship.

When you make someone your primary relationship, you give up everything for the other person. In my teens I was good at sports. I loved going to the beach and surfing. Then when I met my first girlfriend, I gave up all these fun things to be with her all the time. I gave up being me to have her. This is what I had done in my relationship with Nash as well. If you make your kids your primary relationship they have to look to you as the source of their life, and everything you choose, you choose for them. You are not in the picture.

Expecting my son to be my savior made it so I could never find the space to be me or to be happy. Is it ever your child's job to make you happy?

I left the relationship with Nash's mother when he was four. After struggling as a single parent on-and-off for four years, I made a demand that my life change. Two weeks later, I found an advertisement in the newspaper saying, "All of life comes to me with ease, joy and glory. Call Mel." This was how I found Access Consciousness®.

I booked a session with Mel and she started doing

something called The Bars®. I laid down on a massage table and sobbed for an hour while she asked me some questions. "What's going on with you? What's happening in your life? What's not working for you?" I told her things that I had never told anyone. I let all my walls down. She asked me more questions and offered me some pragmatic tools.

After the session with Mel, I got in my car and didn't start it for about 10 minutes; I just sat there. It was the first time I felt truly happy in my whole life.

## Morning Meltdown

Before I found Access, I would wake up every morning and go through a routine I called, "The Morning Meltdown." Step 1: judge myself. Step 2: make myself wrong. Step 3: think about everything that made me unhappy. Step 4: wonder why I could not get anything right... and so on. No one had ever explained that I was so aware, I was capable of picking up the thoughts, feelings and emotions of everyone around me.

To me, awareness is far greater than psychic ability; it is a sense of everything. I had always assumed that if I could think a thought or feel sad then it had to be mine. Everything that was going through my world—thinking, feeling, sensing, hearing—had to be mine. Whose else could it be?

Who Does This Belong To?

One of the first tools of Access is: "Who does this belong to?" When I began asking this question for anything that showed up, the constant mind chatter started to go away. The pains in my body went away. My depression and unhappiness went away. Where was this tool when I was a child? And what could it create for our own children if we gave them this tool to use for themselves?

## Questions?

I began to ask questions about everything. Rather than concluding what was wrong with me, I would ask, "What's right about me?" Instead of saying, "This sucks," I would ask, "How does it get any better than this?" Feeling like crap soon turned into, "Who does this belong to?" I used these three questions all of the time. My life was changing. The joy and wonder I always knew was possible started showing up. I had no doubt that these tools were working.

One of the things I started asking for was more ease with parenting. I mean, where is the instruction manual that was supposed to come with my son? Instead of trying to come up with the answers, I started asking questions.

When Nash started school every day, it was a fight to get him there and he would come home unhappy. At first I thought, *"Well this is school and he will get used to it."* Wait a minute! What if I asked some questions? So I asked Nash, "What would you like to change here? Would you like to find a different school?" He answered with a most definite, "YES." So we asked, "What would it take for a school to show up that would be fun and nurturing for you?" Within one week we found a school that was five minutes' drive from our house that we had no idea even existed. He signed up and has been there ever since. He loves it and now school is fun for him. That one question changed his life. I wonder what else we could ask for?

## Getting it Right

I was always trying to get parenting right. Every choice I considered was first met with the thought, *"Is this the right choice or the wrong choice?"*

What if parenting isn't something you can get right?

I realized that when I tried to get parenting right I ended up judging myself. It always put me back in that trap. The purpose of judgment is to destroy—it doesn't create. What if you were willing to be the worst parent on the planet? This doesn't mean you will be a bad parent, but that willingness can give you the freedom to choose what would actually work for you and your children.

After Nash was born, I decided that I would not treat him like my dad had treated me. I thought if I could just do the opposite of everything my dad had done then maybe I would get it right. Whenever you try hard not to be like someone, or to do the opposite of what they did, you become even more like them. It's like when you find yourself saying the very same things to your kids that your mum and dad said to you!

When you find yourself reacting, ask yourself, "Who am I being? If I was being me right now what would I choose?" Instead of hating my father and blaming him for the way he treated me, I now realize that he did what he could with the tools he had at the time. After all, I had chosen him as my parent.

## Creation

Years ago I heard in an Access Consciousness class that where you are in your life today is a direct result of all the choices you have made up to that point. This got me to see that I am in the driver's seat and in total control of what I am creating in my life. Creation isn't just important as a parent, it's vital for simply being on this planet. If I'm feeling funky, tired or down, I ask myself, "What can I create right now?" or, "Where do I need to put my energy now?" The awareness I get from asking those questions allows me to move forward in my life. Creation allows us to grow. As soon as you define yourself as a parent, creation will stop. Don't define. Instead ask, "Who would I like to create myself as today?" It's amazing how quickly the funk turns around.

## Choice

I started to teach Nash about choice. He would ask me questions about things and rather than tell him what I thought, I would ask him, "What would you like to choose?" about everything. To me, choice is simply putting one foot in front of the other. I don't make it significant. One thing I do in the morning is ask, "What next?" A million things come up and I then look at what would I like to choose right now, rather than conclude that I need to choose how my whole life is going to look forever.

Nash came to me one day and said he was going to live with his mum. It was not, "I am going to live with my mum and I will see you on weekends" or, "I'll see you in a couple of weeks." That day, I wondered what I had done wrong. Then I realized he was making a choice that, for whatever reason, worked for him. He was using the tools I had shown him. I have learned that if you teach your kids about choice, you need to let them choose whatever it is they need to choose. As my wonderful friend Dain Heer says, "Choice creates awareness, awareness does not create choice."

## Start Fresh Each Day

If yesterday didn't exist, what would you create with your kids? Destroying and un-creating your relationship with your kids every day allows you to create from the present and not look to the past as a source for your future. This doesn't mean you will lose your connection with your children. Rather, it gives you that place where you start fresh each day. Don't ever hold grudges. If they made a mistake don't make it mean anything; kids function from the now. Are you willing to function like that as a parent?

## Bullying

As a kid I got bullied and bullied and never did anything to anyone. When I got picked on, I thought I was wrong and bad, and that the bullies were better than me.

I would go home crying and my mum would say, "You have to stand up for yourself." One day when I was 14, some kids started whipping me with long grass. That day, they stepped over the line and I punched one of them in the face, really hard. Everyone in the playground saw it and saw me as someone they did not want to mess with, ever. Violence is never the answer, but I had gotten to a point where enough was enough. I was willing to do whatever it took to end the bullying.

As a parent, you want to go and kick ass, but always look at what is going to create more for your child. You have to let your kids go through whatever they need to go through to get the awareness for themselves of, "This doesn't work for me. This will never work for me. I need to change this."

What if you could teach your kids to be the energy that no one would want to mess with? Teach your kids that they are valuable. Are you willing to be controlled by people? What if you, being the energy of, *do this again and you'll regret it*, taught your kids to stand up for themselves and take control of their own lives?

## Money

As a kid I would ask my parents, "How much did this cost?" and they would say, "It's none of your business." I would insist, "But how much did this house cost?" The reply was always, "None of your business," so I thought money was none of my business. I took this attitude into adulthood. After leaving home and getting a place of my own, I would not open bills when they arrived. I figured if I didn't actually see the bill it would just go away.

Later, when I got into relationship, if I made money my girlfriend would spend it. Or, because I didn't want her to spend it, I would spend it first. I never saw money as something I could have. I was not bright on this topic!

Then I heard about this thing called "the 10 percent account." The 10 percent account is where you put away 10 percent of everything you earn as an honoring of you and let it accumulate. I thought it was a ridiculous idea but I did it anyway.

I'd do it for two days, then spend it.

I'd do it for a week, then spend it.

Then I would do it for a month, and spend it.

I realized the trick to this 10 percent account wasn't having money to spend but actually accumulating money. I wondered, if I didn't spend it all, how much money I would actually have? So rather than *trying* to do this again, I made a *demand* to do it. I never spent that money again. As a parent, if you desire to create money in your life, then teach your kids to create money. I went from broke, living week-to-week and having no money in my life ever to actually growing my wealth as a result of my willingness to *have* and not just *spend* money.

One of the things I love about Access is that anything you think is permanent actually isn't. You alone have the power to change your life. Have you ever thought, *I'm broke* and made more money? Have you ever thought, *My life is pathetic* and had a pathetic life? Have you ever thought, *My kids drive me mad* and your kids did exactly that? What if you were the one creating the broke and pathetic in your life? When you are willing to change your point of view, you can change your entire life.

What would you actually like to have in your life? What kind of clothes? What kind of job? What kinds of food do you like? How much money do you require to run the life you would like to have?

When you're willing to look pragmatically at what you would really like, instead of keeping those thoughts to the land of, "I wish," and, "If only I had money," you can start to create it. I let myself look at what I actually liked to have in my life. I then asked, "OK, what do I have to be or do different to have that show up?"

Educate your kids about having money, spending it, earning it and how money works in the world. If your kids go out and earn money, let them spend it on whatever they like and not on what you think is best. Let them be in control of their choices with it.

## Play

As a dad, I have tried it all. I tried serious parenting. I tried reading-the-books parenting. I tried listening-to-everyone else, and I tried my parent's parenting. None of it worked. Now I use questions: "If I were to be pragmatic, what would I choose? If I were to laugh about every choice I made as a dad, would I be afraid?"

Watch your children. Are they ever serious? Are you willing to have fun with parenting but not allow your kids to walk all over you? Play with these tools; practice them. When your kids are going through stuff and you're not sure what to say, ask yourself, "What could someone have said to me as a kid in this situation that would have made it all ok?" As a parent, it is not your job to create your children through your eyes. It is your job to give them the tools to create themselves through their own eyes.

# About the Author

BRENDON WATT

Brendon is a "Dad with a Difference." His approach to parenting is one of empowerment, choice, contribution and question, and he would like to offer you the possibility of a completely different reality with your children. For many parents, struggle and sacrifice are their daily routine and glimpses of joyful freedom can be scarce. Brendon has changed what once was a difficult burden into a dynamic and easy exchange with his child. He now has more space to be him by allowing and watching his son grow into his own.

Now he and his son travel the world creating lives filled with joy and ease. Brendon is an international speaker on the subject of "Totally Different Dad" and is continuing to make a difference in the lives of many families. You can find out more about his work at www.totallydifferentdad.com.

# Chapter 7

## Cultivating the Joy of Embodiment

### By Cathleen Connor

Can you take yourself back in time to when you were small enough to still totally enjoy and sense your body? Do you recall how much you liked to touch, taste, smell, sense, allow and enjoy your body and it's connection with the world around you? I'm aware that this was different for all of us depending on our childhoods, but can you get a sense of your young body's awareness? What age were you when you started shutting down that yumminess of aliveness and communion with your body, other people's bodies, and the Earth? Would you like to allow and actively cultivate something different for your children? What if one of the primary reasons we are here is to fully enjoy conscious embodiment?

I was a child when children were still encouraged to run and play without much structure. We spent hours with our neighborhood friends, playing both unstructured games and tried-and-true games like Capture the Flag or SPUD. Otherwise we were swimming at a community pool, biking to the park or wandering in the neighborhood. I was also fortunate to have parents that were generally not fearful about us venturing freely into the woods, playing in the cornfields or enjoying getting wet in the creek. As we grew, my Dad encouraged us to learn how to enjoy wildlife through canoeing and hiking in nature. My Mom allowed us to play outside for hours around our neighborhood. In this sense, I had more exposure to the natural world than some kids currently do. I'm grateful that this connection lingered for me into adulthood.

Since our bodies are natural sensors of the Earth and all living things, it can be such a nice contribution to kids to have this connection be acknowledged. When we allow communion with all the living things around us, what does that create for ourselves and the kids we know? How can you nurture this for your kids? I've noticed that when I speak out loud my gratitude for the natural world, it brings it more present for my kids. When I'm outside, I mention what's going on for my body. "Feeling the breeze on my skin feels lovely... I love sunshine on my face... Swimming is such a refreshing experience... I can't wait to skip some stones on the water... I'm grateful for the beautiful sunset." Acknowledging the interaction of your body with the world around it can bring your child's awareness to it more fully. Also, letting your children know that they can expand their energy fields out way beyond their body is an easy way to invite them to sense the world around them.

On other matters of the body, and being aware of my body, my upbringing was more typical. My parents had good intentions, and they were doing their best to help me fit into the American culture and some of its norms. As a parent, I myself repeated some similar things with my own twist with my children thinking that I was being a "good" parent. This changed as I became more conscious myself and was made aware of some tools, questions and techniques from Access Consciousness®. What if our bodies were meant to be enjoyed and teach us about our own consciousness and awareness? How can we allow our children to gain their own awareness with their bodies and stay in communication with them? Even though we all have defining moments in our lives where energetically we might start shutting down our enjoyment of our bodies or come up with judgments of our bodies, what are ways that we can prepare our children to stay aware of the conscious choices that they have with their bodies? How can they keep their body's natural, generative energies flowing?

One of the most basic tools is encouraging and allowing curiosity and questions for kids and teens and their bodies. Instead of teaching children that body sensations only fit a strictly cause-and-effect cycle, we can show them how to always be in communication and question with their body. This allows children to gain their own body awareness. For example, many people have been taught to believe that when they gain or lose weight, the cause is what they ate or how much they exercised when there are many other energetic reasons as well. Have you ever "taken on the weight of the world"? How do you suppose this might show up in your body? Have you eaten a high-calorie food that was really yummy for your body and not gained weight from it? Stepping out of the cause and effect scenario of this reality can be so enlightening in terms of communicating with our bodies. If they can understand that their body is a primary way to be aware of their environment— sensory awareness unit—and it's consciousness is required to stay healthy, thriving and happy, could they more effectively be the leader of their own life in a more conscious way? If they get a sense of what is light or expansive along with what's heavy or contractive, they then know they can ask their body questions all of the time. If you as a parent model gratitude for your body and appreciate all messages and sensations as information to be used to gain awareness, your kids can be allowed to experience their body as their primary life partner.

If children learn early that their body is aware of and is interacting with the bodies around them, it can support them to not be in conclusion about their body's sensations. Many cultures tend to honor feelings and emotions without teaching their youth about the difference between perceiving and feeling. If children live with someone who is often angry, they may be perceiving anger and thinking it belongs to them when it doesn't. When a parent is depressed or anxious, a child often takes that on as his/hers as well. If they are taught as soon as possible to ask, "Who does this belong to?" knowing that their body perceives the thoughts, feelings, emotions and sometimes body pains of the people in their environment, they can often move through changes in their body much more effectively. When they are expressing something or acting agitated, if we ask, "What are you perceiving?" or "What are you aware of here?" it allows them to sense how their body interacts with and mimics others.

For example, at school one day I walked into a classroom to talk to a student. When I squatted down to speak to him, I felt a sharp pain in my knee. Instead of assuming it was mine, I remembered to ask, "Who does this belong to?" Even though you don't need to know the answer to that to allow it to return to sender, I noticed that I was in a classroom with a teacher who had just had knee surgery. I thanked my body for the information and asked my body to dissipate the energy that it used to create the mimicking sensation, and the pain went away.

What if our bodies are aware of the Earth and its changes? Sometimes when we notice body sensations or pain, we can be tuned into the Earth changes or stressors. Once again, if children learn that their body's awareness extends to everything around them, they can know to ask questions. Is my body sensing the Earth? If so, what energy can I contribute to the Earth to shift and change this? If you ask them what they are aware of on a regular basis, it gives them a chance to honor and become even more aware of their body's knowing instead of judging it. Plus, there is no right or wrong answer. The questioning brings up a chance to notice what that child can be aware of, a chance to think outside of what has been taught by this culture. You may be surprised at what your children notice or observe when you ask them questions.

In regards to eating and food choices for each individual body, this type of body awareness can be developed in various ways. Depending on their age, you can show them how to check in with their body and it's language to become more clear on what's a "yes" and what's a "no" in their body's communication. Since the body's language is often not in words, they can learn to ask questions and sense what they notice from their body.

For example, when asking my body about food, generally my body will tip forward when it would like to eat or ingest something and tip backwards when it's response is a "no." When I'm checking on amounts of food or drink, I ask my body to give me signals or sensations when it has had enough. For me, sometimes after only half of a glass, the wine will start to taste unpleasant or more like vinegar. So, as a parent, you can put a variety of food out and tell your child to check in with their body about what food will be most nurturing or satisfying. You can model what works for you when you communicate with your body, and/or allow them to find their own way. Sometimes they need to gain awareness in ways that may seem uncomfortable for a parent.

Overeating candy that has them feel sick to their stomach may be one way they learn how to follow their body's signals. Sometimes when a body "feels" hungry, it is aware of other people being hungry. When I'm in a restaurant or eating around other people, it's much easier for me to eat more than my body would normally desire. I've learned that overeating is a way that I "stuff" my own awareness of the energy of others instead of keeping my barriers down and being willing to let myself notice and be in allowance of it all. Once children know that their body sensations sometimes belong to the people around them, it can be helpful to not overeat as much. Many parents encourage their kids to eat when they aren't hungry or to finish food because we have deemed it "healthy" but does this allow children to become tuned in to what their body requires? Can you allow them to choose and create their own awareness and communication with their body?

Some other questions we can teach our kids to ask when energy or uncomfortable sensations come up for them are: What is this? What can I do with it? Can I change it? If so, how? Invite them to see that they are not looking for a "right" answer, but whatever "knowing" that their body can communicate with them. As mentioned above, when certain energy makes me uncomfortable and I'm tempted to overeat, I now know to ask some questions about what else I can choose. When I ask these questions, sometimes my body gives me a picture or sensation to let me know that it would like to take a walk, sit in the grass of my yard, get a hug, take a break etc. If I follow this, I can often shift the energy to treat my body with more honor.

Bodies tend to really enjoy some kind of movement. If we show kids that there are many ways to move our body that might nurture it, it can give them more choices. Some kids love organized sports and others would rather do something like rock climbing, playing in nature or dancing. How can they become more aware of how their body likes to move? Instead of imposing exercise or interactions with others on them, we can ask questions like, "Would your body like to run, walk, dance or something else? Does your body desire rest or some movement now? Does your body like being around that person?" Giving them as many possibilities of different kinds of ways to move and enjoy their bodies can give kids the sense of what works for their body over time. Anywhere we can give them choice and chances to check in with, question and have gratitude for their body, can allow them to experience what it is to honor their body and enjoy embodiment.

How can we allow our kids to mature into sexual beings without having to take on shame, guilt and blame and relationships that are harmful? Based on my culture's messages, I developed some posture problems by high school since I felt like I needed to hide my chest as it developed. What else is possible? Encouraging our kids to enjoy their developing bodies, without shutting down the natural, generative energy that goes with this, can support them in choosing to be who they are in public without taking on others' ideas about how they should look or be. We can also teach them to be aware of their body signals about who would be nurturing and who would be abusive or unkind. If they become aware that often the people we are attracted to are not always the most kind, nurturing ones, they can learn to ask their bodies questions about people in their world. If their body is giving them a sense that it's not safe or nurturing to be around some people, let them honor that as best as you can. If we hear or sense them starting to judge their body, we can go back to asking, "Who does that belong to?" or, "Who are you being when you judge your body?" If they get the sense that judgment keeps them from tuning into their body's knowing and communication, they can make different choices. Can they find out from their body what it would like to look like and how to create that?

Overall, anywhere that we as parents can keep from imposing our beliefs or concepts on our kids about what we think they should do, while providing a safe environment for them to ask questions and gain their own awareness, can provide the space for them to discover their own knowing. With strong connection and communication with their bodies, children are equipped with a strong guidance tool for life. Their body can give them signals and information that they wouldn't have access to through cognitive channels. If they can stay in total curiosity, wonder, and gratitude with their bodies, it can allow a sense of joy with embodiment that not many people have. Hopefully, parents and children can learn together to create more in this regard by asking each other questions.

The ideas in this chapter are just a beginning. They are inspired from the work of Access Consciousness where people learn to know that they know. What are you aware of with your body, the bodies around you, and the Earth that you can share with your child? How can you have a joyful experience playing with these questions with your child and making up your own? Are you willing to have more joy with your body than most people you know? How about playing with these tools and contacting me to share your feedback and experiences? Thanks for stepping into the JOY of embodiment!

# About the Author

CATHLEEN CONNOR

Being a parent, teacher and Access Consciousness® Facilitator of adult classes, has shaped Cathleen in dynamic ways. Playing in education for 25 years as a Special Education Teacher, she has empowered and learned from students from Pre-Kindergarten to 5th grade. Cathleen has much experience with students with classifications such as ADD/ADHD, Autism, OCD, and Specific Learning Disabilities. She has supported students to look beyond their "label" to become aware of their unique gifts, capacities, strengths and talents. She has also educated and empowered their parents to look at their children from their strengths and enable them to move through school with more ease and less judgment.

Cathleen has over 20 years of parenting experience as well. Learning as she goes, she likes to see what questions she can ask to keep her own judgments of what parenting "should" be out of the way to allow awareness and growth. She is raising two very different and unique sons, who both have taught her about the joys and challenges of parenting.

Cathleen is also an Access Consciousness Certified Facilitator and Body Process Facilitator. After hosting the *Growing up Conscious* Radio Show, she is now co-hosting another radio show called *Super Scoop of Consciousness* on A2zen.fm where she shares the tools of Access Consciousness with people of all ages. As an Access Consciousness Facilitator, she gets to facilitate workshops for children and adults, giving people the tools to know what they know and create conscious change in their lives with ease.

# Chapter 8

## Coloring Outside the Lines

By Trina Rice, OTR/L, MBE

If you had to choose a color of crayon in the box to represent YOU, what color would you be?

Black, white, red, blue or gray? Are you tranquil turquoise? Sunbeam yellow? Outrageous orange? Puke green? Would you be rainbow-striped, tie-dyed or polka-dotted? Is the color of your crayon even inside the box?

Or are you the brightest color of crayon outside the box?

I wonder what our world would of be like if we all colored outside the lines and allowed ourselves to be the brightest colors we could be and shine with infinite possibilities?

I consider myself one of the lucky ones. I get to engage, interact, and connect with children who have been labeled with so-called learning disabilities, special needs, and developmental disorders. Sometimes they are also called the misfits, the trouble-makers and the oddballs.

I like to call them my shining stars; the bright sparkling colors of the crayon box; the gifted, the talented, the wave makers, the Superheroes, and what Access Consciousness® likes to call, "the X-Men."

You see, they have these extra powers; expansive talents and abilities. Yet they are often seen as not belonging, being needy, having a limitation and generally as a wrongness. What if they actually have something unique and different to bring to our lives and to the planet? Many of the so-called misfits, those with some form of disability, are the ones who have been the greatest catalysts for change

When you acknowledge these kids and look at them, not from the wrongness of them, but from what is right about them, you can open up a completely different world for yourself, for them and for everyone on the planet. I am so grateful for how these brilliant beings have allowed me to continually expand my perception, my knowing, and my ability to see things differently. I feel so fortunate to have these kids as my teachers, my mentors, and my playmates. They keep me on my toes, keep me asking for more and inspire me to be the greatest that I can truly be.

Yes, I do have those days when I wake up and I feel like an elephant is sitting on my head or somebody just dropped a ton of bricks on my body, and there are days when these amazing beings don't seem to be so sparkly and bright. It is often at those times that I acknowledge them and their bodies.

These kids do not always have ease with their bodies, yet they are happy to be alive and they have a sense of joy that does not go away. I am not saying they do not have rough moments. They do. However, there is this underlying current of complete joyful happiness that they continue to be even on the crappy days, just like the birds who continue to sing even if they're having a bad feather day and the crickets who continue to chirp even when the sun is not shining.

They have a sense of being; a space, and a wonderment. They have an amazing awareness and communion with everyone and everything... the earth and beyond. "Being" is something we don't have much on this planet. We have "beingness," which is *doing* to *be*. Most of us do a whole lot of doing. One of the gifts that these kids have given me is the ability to BE.

They have an ability to BE in different spaces, different places, different times, and different realities all at the same time. Whether they are listening to music while watching a movie on the television while looking at pictures on their iPad, all while flicking a sock and fidgeting with their hands, or they are running across the room while looking out of the peripheral vision into a vast space, they can all BE.

For most of these gifted children there is no separation of past, present or future. It all exists here and now. It's all oneness. They are aware of all the quantum entanglements; how everything in the universe is interconnected. They can touch a piece of furniture or a book and instantly become aware of everyone who has previously touched it. They can be shown a picture of a ball or hear the word "ball" and every ball that they've ever seen or been in contact with immediately comes into their awareness.

I wonder what would be different if we allowed ourselves to be as aware as they are, as aware of the oneness and the quantum entanglements that exist among us? Just suppose they see something, know something, and be something that we have not been willing to perceive, know, be or receive? What if we changed our perceptions to acoustical perceiving?

Awareness is an acoustical vibration. Acoustical is a state of being. When you are acoustical and willing to BE, you have more capacity to perceive and know what *is*. Being acoustical allows you to be everything that you are. It gives you the freedom to choose without judging, without projecting, without concluding. This space of no judgment, no projections, no conclusions, no limitations and total communion, is the acoustical wave. It is the "acoustical vibration" of what the X-Men *BE*.

Awareness is like the wind that touches your skin and moves on. It is ever changing, never blowing exactly the same. Sometimes it's a soft cool breeze other times it's like a sudden gust of hot air. When the wind blows on your skin, you receive information contained within the breeze. An acoustical vibration is like a wavelength that delivers this information, and you, as an infinite being, have all these waves available. You can perceive the wind on your skin and know if it is a soft cool breeze or if it is a gust of hot air. However, we have learned to transfer this acoustical vibration, which is total awareness, and solidify it into thoughts, feelings and emotions instead of perceiving, knowing, being and receiving.

We have a tendency to make these gifted children wrong for not feeling, thinking or experiencing emotions like we do and many have concluded that they do not understand or even get the concept of emotions. What if they have way surpassed that? What if *they* are not the ones that are deficient? What if instead, they possess capacities *we* haven't evolved to have yet? And, what are they gifting us that we have not been willing to receive or acknowledge? What if we were actually willing to transcend the need to function from thoughts, feelings and emotions? When we do not allow ourselves to receive the acoustical vibration of our awareness with no point of view, we are unable to expand beyond what we already think we know. These kids are different... and we try to make them not be the difference they truly be.

The X-Men are extremely aware of the space 360 degrees all around them, all the time. They are the ones that hear the fire truck sirens miles away, the jet plane flying through the sky, the telephone ringing and the person knocking at your door many minutes before it even shows up in your world. That is living as an acoustical vibration with no separation. It is being in total communion with the quantum entanglements of perceiving, knowing, being and receiving.

You know those times when things just fall into place instantaneously as if by magic and everything works out? Or you think of someone and the phone rings and it is them on the other line? That is the acoustical wave. We can ride on this acoustical wavelength when we get out of our judgments, decisions, conclusions, projections and limitations.

I remember standing in front of a large audience, trembling as I spoke about an experience I had while working with a child who was having a seizure. I recall the child's stare penetrating into my eyes as if to say, "Please help me," as his body was thrashing on the floor. I asked the child, "What is it that you require?" Not knowing nor expecting to get an answer from the child, I was willing to perceive an energy, an energetic communication of what it was that he required. While he was reaching out for my hands, I proceeded to ask the child, "Where do you need my hands to be placed on your body?" I placed one hand on his chest and the other on the top of his head. I then asked to be the contribution that was required for him. I asked the molecules of his body to shift, to change, to turn and to create an ease within his body. In less than a minute the child was laughing. His eyes were gleaming and his skin was glowing again.

It was not until I was sharing this experience with the group that I realized: none of what occurred was cognitive, nor was the communication verbal. I was *being* the acoustical wave where the molecules of our bodies were able to vibrate and change, allowing space for a different possibility to show up, without judging or projecting or even concluding what was required. Once I perceived, received and acknowledged what occurred in that experience, I began to understand how it is that I have communicated with these Superheroes, these X-Men, that I never could quite figure out before. When you are willing to be present, to be the space of no separation, no judgment and in total allowance, you are able to ride on the acoustical wave and an energetic exchange occurs between you and the child in front of you, as well as all the energies around you.

These Superheroes-of-magnitude, these extra gifted X-men, have a new playground of possibilities where magic does exist because they have the freedom to choose to be different, without judging. They have this super-duper infinite slide that you can ride on. It is like a magic carpet ride. The slide has no edges, has lots of curves and a few bumps, but is the most spacious slide I have ever experienced and it is never ending. That is what it's like riding on the acoustical wavelength. That is being the acoustical vibration. And that is the language they speak; an energetic communion along the acoustical wave length.

One of the wave makers, an X-man that I get to work with, shared his wisdom and explained this energetic communion that exists beyond words. By typing on his iPad, this is what he communicated:

"I get mad when others
Don't hear me talk
And say and think
That I'm stupid because
I do not talk.

We should not have to use words
To express ourselves.
Get over it.
Be aware.
Be smart.
And listen to the
Vast space
Very loud
Just as I did from right now."

What if you were willing to be the vast space, the energetic connection along the acoustical wavelength? Would you really like to walk through this world, through this reality, without all the confinements, labels, disabilities, limitations and boxes? Are you are willing to choose the acoustical vibration? Then maybe you could walk through walls or slide through space. Are you willing to be different and ride the ongoing waves of possibilities? Are you willing to go on the magic carpet ride?

Are you wondering how you ride on this acoustical wavelength and be the vast space? Let me start by saying, it is not about "how." It is about allowing yourself to *be*; to be who you truly are without all of the projections, expectations, decisions and conclusions of how it works and what you need to do. If you were truly being you, who would you be? Then just be that energy without thinking how to be it.

I have known that I have a connection with these kids but never quite understood what that connection was or how it was created. I just knew that wherever I was, kids would always turn and look at me, even in the midst of chaotic situations. I also could walk into a room and even the child who would not typically make eye contact would look up, stop the present activity or run towards me. I finally realized that I created this sense of connection, space, communion and presence that allowed kids to have a sense of comfort, ease and security.

I was able to show up without judging them, without projecting onto them. I was able to look at them and see beyond the limitations, disabilities and labels, and notice their true essence. This space is referred to as "the zone." The zone allows a sense of calmness and comfort. It is an honoring of who they are, where they are, what they be and what they know.

Sometimes these amazing X-Men have been saturated with projections, expectations and conclusions of who they are and what they can and cannot do based on the labels, diagnoses and the disabilities that they have been given. These labels do not have to be told to them verbally in order for them to pick up these judgments energetically from people's thoughts. They perceive those judgments and often times contract their zone into a constricted space which puts them in a computed box. It's like being inside of a crayon box with only black and white colors.

This can show up in a multitude of ways depending on the child. You may see a child completely shut down, quiet, extremely reserved and hardly ever making a social connection. It may also be displayed as temper tantrums and/or aggressive behaviors. It may be displayed more as an anxious behavior, like wringing their hands, pinching their own skin, biting their fingers or hand. They may have an irritation from wearing certain textures of clothing or be very sensitive to tactile input and touch if it is not initiated by them. This is not a complete list nor is it to say that any and all of those behaviors are due to only a collapsed zone; it is to give an example of some of the indicators that can alert you.

Sometimes a child can be overwhelmed by all of the information they receive and perceive from everyone and everything all around them as there is no separation from the past, present or future for them. They typically do not have the ability to limit or filter the information that they perceive and receive, including all the thoughts feelings and emotions from everyone and everything 360 degrees around and beyond them.

For them, it's like walking into an extremely crowded shopping mall during holiday times without the ability to filter any of the information. There is the glare of all the lights, the shine off the floor, the blaring music, the voices of everyone, the ringing of phones, the dinging of cash registers, the aroma of all the food, the scents of everyone surrounding them and the touch of a million different textures incoming all at once.

These are the times when you can assist them in expanding their zone, pulling out and expanding their space to dissipate the contraction. I begin with saying, "Hi!" Sometimes I verbally say, "Hi," and other times it is more of an energetic, "Hi." I push down all my barriers or walls of what my day may have been, let go of the judgments and projections of who I am and who they are, and I vastly expand my own space. Sometimes I'm just outright silly with them, getting them to laugh.

It is like being in a state of wonder. I become present with them in this space of wonder and acknowledge them for who they are, exactly how they are. It is like energetically sharing, "Wow! You are amazing and awesome just the way you are. I appreciate you. You're welcome to join me and play in my space anytime and I will give you whatever space you require."

This allows them to meet you where you are and allows you to perceive where they are, where their zone exists. Then you can assist them in expanding their zone to a space where they can relax. It is like reaching into their zone and pulling out the edges, pushing down the walls, opening the box and expanding their space. You will see their bodies relax. They may take a big breath, sigh, make eye contact with you, wiggle their bodies into a more comfortable position or even laugh.

Allowing them to perceive and acknowledge this expanded space lets them interact with their environment and others with more ease, comfort and peace. I often times ask them to hold the space so they can begin to perceive when their zone has been squashed or collapsed. It is the start of them acknowledging what they can change to create more ease for themselves.

Sometimes X-men kids are so expanded that they have no connection or limited connection to their bodies. They appear to be off in a faraway land as if in a constant state of daydreaming. I apply the zone technique with them as well. However, it is more of "meeting them where they are."

If I am desiring to connect and interact with them, I vastly expand my zone and become present with them. I ask them, "Where are you?" Then I perceive energetically where they *be*, and it's not a "figuring out." It is just asking the question and following the energy. Many times you are already there even if you think that you are not aware of anything. I may have to state their name and ask, "Where are you?" a few times, but they will eventually become present. They will typically make eye contact with you, even if it is only for a fleeting moment. You may notice a shift with their body. I usually get an absurd glance of, "What did you just say to me?" or, "How did you know where I was at?" Then I ask them, "What if you could stay there and also be here with me?" Most of the time they then become present with you. You are allowing them to be who they are, where they are, and be with you all at the same time. You are not limiting them to only being in the space beside you. You are allowing them to be everywhere.

It is a gift and an invitation that is different than what they have been presented with before. It is the gift of allowing them to be who they are, acknowledging them for how they show up without judgments, asking questions and allowing them to shine as the brightest color outside of the box.

What if you did not have to figure it out? What if you could ask questions, follow your awareness and your knowing, and make choices? What if that is what is required to be the brightest color of crayon outside the box? I wonder what our world would be like if we all colored outside the lines and allowed ourselves to shimmer and shine in all of our glory and all of our greatness?

What if these X-Men, the Superheroes-of-magnitude, the wave makers are the brightest colors and shine with infinite possibilities? What if they are assisting in dissipating all the perceived separation between us, between others, between us and the earth, and the greatness we can truly be? What if they are the keys to unlocking the separation beyond words, beyond constructs, beyond limitations, beyond conclusions to a space of total communion?

Are you willing to be tie-dyed or have polka-dots? Are you willing to be the rainbow-striped crayon? Are you willing to add some shine, sparkle and dazzle? What if you were the shimmering multicolored crayon outside the box, riding on the magic carpet ride of ongoing waves of possibilities?

# About the Author

TRINA RICE, OTR/L, MBE.

Trina Rice, OTR/L, MBE., CFMW is the owner of Harmony Therapeutics, LLC., has over 18 years of experience as an Occupational Therapist working with kids of all ages, including adults and families of all kinds. She is known to have a great connection with children, particularly those with special abilities. She has the ability to see kids and adults for the amazing capacities that they have, beyond any limitations, disabilities, diagnosis or labels.

She blends traditional Occupational Therapy training with manual therapy techniques, including Craniosacral Therapy, Myofascial Release, massage and Access Consciousness® tools and processes...with a splash of fun added in. Trina brings allowance and play into her work, along with self-discovery and gentleness.

Trina is a licensed Occupational Therapist, has a Master's in Bio-Energetics and is an Access Consciousness Certified Facilitator and Access Consciousness Body Process Facilitator, along with several certifications in many other body work practices.

In between running, planting flowers, and cosplaying as a Superhero for charity events and comic-cons, Trina enjoys facilitating private sessions for kids and adults in person, and over phone or Skype. She loves traveling, enjoying our Earth and facilitating Access Consciousness Bars®, Body Process and Core classes around the globe.

Trina is a host on the weekly A2zen.fm internet-based radio show, *Super Scoop of Consciousness*, dedicated to discovering your own superhero-of-magnitude and the brilliance of you. The archives, upcoming shows and more can also be found on the *Super Scoop of Consciousness* Facebook page and on iTunes Podcast. Trina has a story published in the book *Would You Teach a Fish to Climb a Tree?* and also has more stories to share in upcoming books.

Connect with Trina:

www.trinarice.accessconsciousness.com

Facebook~ Trina Rice www.facebook.com/trina.rice.180

Facebook~ Harmony Therapeutics www.facebook.com/accesstrinar/?fref=ts

What if YOU were the light bulb that allowed inspiration to shine on others when you walked into a room? What if you being YOU is what is required to change the world??

BE the POSSIBILITY. BE DIFFERENT. BE YOU!!!

# Chapter 9

## What Do Kids Need Most from a Parent?

By Mary Dravis-Parrish

What if there is one thing that kids would like their parents to be? Do they want them to control them? To project fear into their lives? To hold expectations that may or may not be realistic? To judge every choice they make in the hopes that all of this will make the child successful and motivate them to do good in the world? Has this been the model for parents for way too long? How well is this working? Is there another possibility that might allow both the parent and the child to experience life in a different, more empowering way?

You might say, "My kids just want me to love them. That is all that they really need." And most people would agree with that. The word "love" carries many different meanings and people have had it expressed in a variety of ways that may or may not be what your kids would like from you. Perhaps you had experiences of love that didn't meet your needs or didn't feel like your definition of love. So let's put the love component aside for now. What else might kids want from their parents?

I have been sharing with parents a concept called **Be YOU Parenting**™, whereby parents have the opportunity to parent their children from within their own empowered knowing and being. They parent with the capacity and the desire to guide and nurture their kids through life without control, expectations, judgments, separations or projections. Parents look inward to acknowledge the experiences in their own lives where they have defaulted to creating their life based on the requirements of someone else, including points of view about parenting. Tools are offered that support and bring about the change that is desired. Fortunately, raising children offers parents plenty of opportunity for such discovery and transformation. Kids will often mirror a parent's worst self image. This is not about moving into judgment of our self image; it is about acknowledging what may be keeping a person from being, doing and having all that they desire in life, including an empowering relationship with their children.

In my book, *Empowered Parents Empowering Kids - A Guide to Be YOU Parenting*, I offer techniques that I have applied from Access Consciousness® that assist parents in identifying who they are being, not only as a parent, but also in all areas of their life. Consider a parent who struggles with fear in her life. Even though her fear is not based on anything real in the moment, like facing a blazing fire or a wild animal, it can feel very real. It may be what keeps that parent from being able to let go of controlling her children. Fear is founded in a lie that is believed to be real. In the book parents learn about fear and how it is based on "what ifs" that project more fear onto children. A fearful parent may find herself telling her child to "be careful" in all situations, which projects onto the child that the world is a place to be feared. When this parent is able to release and let go of the fear that is controlling her life, she can parent from within her true being and her true knowing. She can guide and instruct her child how to be aware of situations and to choose based on awareness and knowing, not out of fear. Parents who are embracing **Be YOU Parenting** are able let go of and move beyond functioning from guilt, fear, worry, doubt, anger, control, and all the other aspects of living that keep them from being able to choose what they desire, which also allows parents to empower their own children to create the life they would like to have as well.

Imagine what your life would be like if no one ever judged you. What would it be like to live your life without judging yourself or others? Judgment distracts a person from being who he would truly like to be. Have you ever stopped yourself from choosing for you because you were afraid of what others would think? Have you made other people's points of view more significant than you? Without meaning to, have you projected these points of view onto your children so that they will do the same? When you let go of the power that judgment has over you, you can step into being in allowance of yourself and your children. All of the controlling, projecting, and expecting can cease as you begin to choose to live your life based on what you would like to be, do and have, instead of validating other people's view of what you *should* be, do or have. Parents can choose to be empowered to stop moving to conclusions about how their kids should live their lives. Both parent and child can move into a world of infinite possibility, where choices are never judged. Each choice gives more awareness and if choice was never judged, how much more aware could one be for future choices?

How much does your child have to gain by making her

own choices? What if your child's choices didn't have any judgment attached to them? How many of your choices from your childhood were judged? Did you learn anything from the choices you made? Would you have learned those things even if the choices weren't judged? Maybe even with more ease, because you wouldn't have made yourself wrong for your choices. Regret, or the sense of feeling bad about previous choices or actions, is what shows up when our choices have been judged as wrong. What if choice is just choice and it doesn't require being judged as wrong or right? We can have a greater awareness in choice when we get out of judgment. What if with each choice we can simply ask a question like, "How is this working for me now?" or "Would I like to keep choosing this or is something else possible?" Leaving the judgment out of it creates more ease and allowance. When parents use this with the choices their kids make, it creates a stronger bond between the parent and child.

People have been ingrained to use judgment as a motivation for change. Praise our kids for what they have done right, punish them for what they have done wrong and they will grow up to fit into the mold of humanity. Fine, except if you were to push the pause button and ask, "How empowering is that?" what is your sense about that? Judgment is judgment, whether it is judging what is good or what is bad. We are trained to seek to be judged as good, and not as bad. What if something else is possible? What if we didn't have to prove that we are good or bad?

Kids grow up looking to others to validate their performance, their choices, and their very existence. Can you relate? Do you still require someone else to tell you that you have done a good job, or made a good choice? When a child is born she is appreciated for her very being and then as she grows she learns that *being* isn't appreciated anymore and you have to *prove* your worth here on this planet through earning positive judgment. What else is possible that will allow a person to be valued just because they exist and are free to be who they choose to be?

**Be YOU Parents** discover that letting go of judgment, fear, guilt and worry creates more harmony in their home. The steps that I offer for moving out of judgment and fear are actually quite simple and yet very profound and life-changing. Using empowering questions can give awareness to a situation. For example, asking the question, "Who does this belong to?" or "Is this (fear, guilt, anger, judgment) mine?" allows a person to begin to see that most of these sensations do not originate with oneself, but have been projected, expected and implanted to the point that they can feel very much a part of who we are. I wonder if the fear and judgment that you project onto your child feels as if it belongs to them? If so, then they may mirror back their fear to you, which is actually your fear that you took on from someone or something else. Thus asking the question brings up the awareness that if it doesn't belong to you, you don't have to continue to own it. It is often easier to tell what isn't yours when you ask the question and you sense that you feel lighter. You can figure that 99.9 percent of the time it isn't going to be yours. Then the choice is there to send it back and to choose something else. It is a simple 4-Step process:

1. Acknowledge that you are experiencing —fear, judgment, guilt, doubt, worry, anger etc

2. Ask —Who does this belong to? Is this mine? You need not know who it belongs to, just that it isn't yours.

3. Clear it away —return it to sender, clear away any aspect you continue to believe it is yours. You may use the Access Clearing Statement. (for info about the clearing statement see www.theclearingstatement.

com)

4. Choose something else. Instead of this _____ I choose to be, do or have _____.

Choice is vital in this process. Choice allows a person to move into *being* what would actually create more for them. It may be to choose joy, fun, awareness, ease, allowance or confidence. The choice is just a choice. The key is that it is the place where a person gets to BE who they choose to be, not what they think is expected. This is the place that kids would like their parents to be —in a place of choosing to BE who they would truly enjoy being.

Empowering questions also remove limitations and the need to have the answer. Asking a simple question like, "What else is possible?" allows limitations to dissolve and possibilities to emerge. What if life were that easy? Would you be willing to step into more ease with living and parenting? Life will continue to be a struggle if one isn't willing for things to be different, such as having more ease. And who does that belong to?

Parents use this question to get out of having to come up with the answer for their kids. They empower their kids to be in question, too. One mother, whose younger son was upset because his older brother wouldn't share a video game with him, came crying and complaining to his mom. Of course, his motive was that his mother was going to fix this for him and he would get what he wanted. She surprised him by asking him, "What else might be possible that you haven't considered?" He offered some more complaints, yet she held firm with, "I just wonder what else might be possible for you." When he saw that she wasn't going to solve this problem for him, he went back to his brother and within 30 seconds, they had it all worked out. I was delighted to have been able to witness this in action with this family. This became an empowering moment for both sons and it created more ease for the parent too.

Now let's come back to the issue about love. If you were *being* you from a place of less judgment, fear, guilt, worry, control, expectation and projection, and more from a place of gratitude and choosing what you would like to be, do or have, would you be in a place to nurture and guide your child in his choices? Would you be in more allowance of who your child chose to be? And would this be what you might refer to as "love"? How much more of you would be present to parent your child? What if all that your child would like from you is for you to *be you*? What if you were a **Be YOU Parent**?

The book *Empowered Parents Empowering Kids - A Guide to Be YOU Parenting* gathers the tools of Access Consciousness and takes the reader on an adventure of collecting tools, insights, and possibilities about creating a life from within the reader's deepest desires to BE and to live from that place of being. The book shares more tools about creating choice, awareness, trust, and allowance that empowers the parent, who then, by the very act of *being* more, can empower their children to be the magnificent, unique, creative being they BE through their own choosing. The adventure of **Be YOU Parenting** is exciting, life changing and full of unexpected thrills. It offers you the one thing that your children need from you-to be who you truly BE!

# About the Author

MARY DRAVIS-PARRISH

 Mary Dravis-Parrish has over 25 years of experience as an educator, trainer, coach, and speaker working with kids and parents to create different possibilities in family living. She brings her 40+ years of parenting experience which includes being a teen parent, a single parent, a co-parent and step-parent as well as a grieving parent after the suicide death of her son. In addition to her son, she has two other sons, a step daughter and a step son.

These parenting challenges, as well as the experiences Mary had growing up in a large family, contributed to Mary discovering, after the death of her son, that her life needed to change. She was ready to let go of being in control of things she couldn't control, like making her family happy, keeping her current husband sober, and judging every choice she made. The guilt she carried about not being there for her son was taking its toll. It was time to find out if this life had anything else to offer. But how could this be possible when she had done all of the things that were supposed to bring you joy, happiness and a fruitful life, and had failed? It is in the surrendering to something else being possible that opened the space for the tools and processes of Access Consciousness® to be introduced to Mary in 2010. Immediately she knew there was something here that would give her what she had been yearning for. As she applied the tools and processes to eliminate her own fears, guilt, worry, doubt, control and anger. She began to discover that she was free to choose to be, do and have the life of her own choosing. She didn't need to have someone else tell her how to live her life.

Mary began to use these tools and strategies with her own parenting as well as introduce them to parents that she worked with in her coaching practice. In her own home, she found that there was more ease as she let go of having to be in control, to be right and to be responsible for any outcome. Her children began to relate to her with more ease. She found she could have more allowance for their choices as they moved into adulthood. As she began to use these tools in her coaching practice, the parents she worked with discovered that they too were feeling less guilt, less pressure, less anxiety and much more joy and confidence. They were experiencing changes in their own life aside from being a parent that allowed them to be more positive about living, creating more of the life they desire to live, following their own dreams, and being empowered to empower their children to be whatever they choose to be, without fear or expectation.

Wanting more parents to have the opportunity to know about these tools, Mary wrote the book *Empowered Parents Empowering Kids - A Guide to Be You Parenting* to encourage and support parents through difficult times; to encourage them to search for a different way of parenting through self discovery and transformation referred to as **Be YOU Parenting**™. The book offers parents permission to see themselves through the eyes of their children, to be transformed to be who they truly be and to be empowered to become the parent that will empower kids. Mary, a certified facilitator with Access Consciousness, now invites parents and children to shed the limitations, judgments and fears associated with family living and step into the allowance, joy, ease and fun of Being YOU. It is a glorious adventure, well worth the trip!

*Empowered Parents Empowering Kids - A Guide to Be You Parenting* can be purchased on Amazon. com as well as the Access Consciousness shop at www. accessconsciousness.com/shop. To learn more about Mary, her services or to bring **Be YOU Parenting** to your area visit: www.BeYouParenting.com.

# Chapter 10

## Being a Question-able Parent

By Dr. Glenna Rice, DPT

When you ask a question and you don't look for an answer it opens doors to access awareness that can contribute to changing anything you are asking to change. It gives you clarity about what is creating limitation in your life and allows for possibilities that can create more than you ever imagined.

Before I began to truly create my life and my family, before I discovered the amazingly pragmatic and magical tools from Access Consciousness®, I was a consummate suburban soccer mom. I had my then 11-year-old son in nearly every activity I could fit into his day—he did soccer, baseball, karate, gymnastics and his homework. My oldest daughter was seven and she was in gymnastics, ballet and karate. My youngest, then 18 months, was being drug around in strollers and car seats from daycare to her sibling's practices. I had also just opened my physical therapy practice, not to mention all the other daily things required to be a good mom in this reality, from meals and cleaning, to driving and homework. Our days were insanely over-scheduled and I was angry, frustrated, and sad, often. The thing is, like many mothers who are reading this, I was able to do everything and do it well, even if I didn't enjoy it. I had all these fixed points of views of what was required to fit into this idea of what being a good mom is. It is as if we mothers are constantly forcing our kids up a steep hill based on what we *should* do while dragging our limited lives on a chain behind us. We are forcing what we think our life should be on ourselves and using tons of control to fit it into this small tiny box of parenting based on the context of this reality.

What if there is something else possible? What if there is a way of being that allows so much more joy, ease and abundance that we are missing constantly, because we can't see out of the box we are forcing ourselves and our children into? The little tiny box of what we think are the right things to do for our kids so they turn out to be "successful." One thing that we never do is ask a question...a questions like "Is this working for me?" or, "What do my children actually require from me?" or, "What would I like to add to my life?"

How did everything change? Ten years ago, during a break at a workshop in Sedona, Arizona, I sat watching this gigantic ant hill. The ants looked so insanely busy running up and running down. I thought, "Wow! That is my life (I live on a hill too). I'm just like these crazy ants running around up and down the hill." Then this awareness struck me: I realized that they were not angry! Right then, I asked the question that started to change everything in my and my children's lives: "What would it take for me to not be so angry all the time?" I did not know what that question would change for me then, but it was truly potent. It opened me up to begin to *become* the question, to start to follow the energy of what was light for me and my family, and I started to have joy in my life for maybe the first time ever!

How the contribution shows up is not something we can logically come up with, but if you allow yourself to open the door to what is possible, from asking the question, then it opens this door for the consciousness of everything to contribute to what you are asking for. The day I asked that question, a friend of mine fell off a stool and injured her back and asked me for a Physical Therapy session. She got such great results she referred a friend to me who just "happened" to be an Access Facilitator! Within a few weeks, that question lead me to the incredible tools of Access Consciousness, which allowed me to begin to access the consciousness I required to change everything that was not working for me by choosing and asking questions. EVERYTHING!!!!

My life is very different now, 10 years later. I am creating all the time. I am busier than I was and I love it and I am not angry all the time. In fact, I have joy in my life... and ease! These are all things I would have never even imagined possible when I was watching that ant hill. The questions I use, or the question I *am* give me the ability to see what is or isn't working in my life; what I would like to add, what I would like to change, and how to change it with such ease. I never ever doubt what I am creating and my children don't either. My life flows and would probably look even crazier and busier now than 10 years ago, but because it is based on awareness and not force, everything just falls into place. Now we float up that hill. We could jump off if we chose to, and know the universe will be there to support us on the ride down. My life is a gift and is full of surprises all the time. How does it get better than that?

Two of the many invaluable tools that have contributed to me and countless parents creating more ease with parenting are knowing that the best protection for your children is awareness, and the willingness to be a bad parent.

## The Best Protection for Your Children Is Awareness

Fear, worry, and concern for your children are considered a valuable way to parent in this reality. This is often how parents prove they care for their children. If you are not worrying about your children you are not considered normal and can be judged as unconcerned and uncaring. Most of us were parented from fear and have never seen that there is a different possibility. The problem is that fear limits you and your children's ability to know what is true. It stops your awareness.

What if there is a different possibility? What would it be like if you could parent without fear? Would it be different than what you are creating now? What could your children generate if you were not afraid for them? If they were not afraid? If they actually had access to what they know? Fear is never real. It is a distraction that keeps you from knowing.

What if you could have easier access to your ability to know that you know?

If you function from awareness, fear cannot exist because you will always know if your children are safe. You will know if your child is going to cross the street safely, or not. You'll be aware of whether or not your teenager is going to be ok going out with their friends. If your child has studied enough for their next exam, or not, you'll know. And you'll also have awareness of whether the future they are creating will be greater than you can imagine for them.

So what is awareness and how do you build the muscle to know that you know?

Awareness, for most of us, is light as a feather. It is often missed in this reality because it is rarely acknowledged and we give much more value to what feels dense and heavy. The density of this reality is "louder" but awareness is much more substantial. The more often it is acknowledged, the more ticklish that feather becomes until it starts to become too difficult to ignore. Every time we acknowledge when we are aware, we become more in tune with the tickle of that feather. When we are grateful for it and ask for more every time we have an awareness, we increase this ability to receive the information we are asking for. If you stop or shut down someone's knowing by simply saying, "You can't know that," or "that is not possible," you disempower them. With each disempowerment they disconnect more and more from their own ability to be aware. A great question to ask is, "How does it get even better than this?" This question allows you to acknowledge something great has shown up and ask for more. It will expand what is possible.

How do you know? You ask a question and then perceive the energy. You do not look for an answer. You perceive what feels light or heavy. If it is light, it is true for you. If it is heavy, it is a lie.

If you are worried for your children, or feel fear, ask a question. "What is this energy? Is my child safe? Yes or no?" What feels light? It actually is that easy! For 10 years now, after first learning this tool in an Access Consciousness class and using it countless times with my three children and teaching this tool to hundreds of parents, it has always worked. Functioning from the question and awareness is a much easier way to parent! You just have to desire it to be that easy.

So much more magic is possible when we do not create the pretense of fear in place of awareness. You want to ask your children to be aware. Do not tell them to be careful. Teach them to be aware-full.

I watched my youngest daughter teach herself how to swim in a few hours when she was three years old by jumping over and over again into the deep end of a pool and wiggling herself back to the side with total joy. When she first jumped I freaked a little, but what she was doing was having fun and enjoying her body. Instead, I expanded my awareness out and asked the question, "Is she safe?" It was a "yes." It was actually so light, I smiled. She did not have my fear to distract her from her knowing, allowing her more awareness of what was possible for her. It was amazing what she created. She taught herself how to swim that day with absolute delight. My children are extremely aware, like your children are, and if we create fear they perceive it and this can override what they already know. What would it take to start creating something different and empower you and your children to know that you know! It is that easy!

## Are You Willing to Be a Bad Mom?

To be a truly great parent you have to be willing to be a "bad" parent. When you are willing to receive the judgments that you are a bad mother or father as just someone's interesting point of view then you can be the phenomenal parent you truly be.

How does this tool work? Once you become a parent, everyone will share with you their judgments about the correct, right and good way to raise your kids. They will give you advice on how to deliver your baby, how to nurse, what to feed your kids, if you should stay home or go back to work, what activities your kids should do, if you should discipline your kids, what college they should go to and on and on. If you make these judgments real at all, you can never see what would actually work for you or for your kids. Instead, you stop being you and discount what you know to avoid their judgments. If you are willing to be a "bad" mom, then any judgments you get from your kids, the neighbors or your mother in-law will not be able to stick you because you are already willing to receive them. You have allowance for what they think and it becomes just an interesting point of view. You never need to resist or react to the judgments and make your choices wrong. You can choose how to parent for you and create something greater than you could imagine.

This tool allows you to never have to fit into this reality's insanity about parenting. Like this insane view: if you are a "good mother" you have to sacrifice your life for your kids. Have you ever heard anyone say, "I would give up my life for my children"? This is supposed to be a good thing? No, it is crazy! What child would want their parent to give themselves up for them? I never wanted that from my mom; I wanted her to be amazing! Giving your life up for your children does not show them how to be phenomenal, it shows them how to be limited. I desire my children to have the choice to be phenomenal. When we as parents choose greater over sacrifice, then we show our children how to choose that for their future, too. In this reality, sacrifice is the "right way" to parent. A "bad parent" would create greater than this.

Are you willing to be a "bad mother" and create a greater life and an amazing future for you and your kids, without sacrificing you?

Sometimes the most difficult judgments to receive are those from our own children. Here are two stories where using this tool created wonderful changes I would never have considered.

Years ago, when they were in elementary school, I put the wrong sandwiches in my daughters' lunch boxes: one got tuna and one peanut butter... and they both hated the sandwiches they got. When I picked them up from school I got a litany of how awful it was for them at lunch. I turned to them and said, "I am sorry. I am a really bad mom. I don't know how to do this stuff right, maybe I need your help." I did not get upset, resist or react to what they were complaining about. The girls both said, "Oh no, you are not a bad mommy at all, you are the best mommy ever!" and started helping make their own lunches.

Recently my 17-year-old daughter had a very difficult day at school and she was seriously down in the dumps. That night, she left the house and didn't tell me. When I found out where she had gone I was not happy. My son, who is 21 now, laid into me about how I was acting. He said, "You are terrible, you are going to get mad at her when she is depressed? What kind of mother are you?" I started to react and argue with him, defend myself, tell him I wouldn't do that, that is not what is going on here. Then I remembered the tool: *be willing to be a bad parent*, be willing to receive his judgments as just an interesting point of view. I expanded out, become more space, and repeated in my head, "What would it take to be willing to be a bad parent? Interesting point of view he has this point of view."

What this changed was amazing. He almost instantly stopped judging me. There was no more space in my world for what he was saying to stick me. The "I have to be a good mom" button was gone. He started to tear up and I asked what was up for him. He started to talk about things that were troubling him about his future. He had been worried that when he finished his degree in engineering he would end up stuck in a job that would be boring, that he hated, and he would become depressed. Wow, that was not where I would have thought the conversation about his sister would go! This opened the door for an amazing, generative conversation full of questions about his future and how to create a future that would work for him. I was able to show him a totally different possibility beyond this reality. I agreed: yes you may end up in a boring engineering job. And when you do, you will change it or get a new job. You can do this as often as you like, just like I did, and just like your dad did. You will never be able to do a boring job, you are too creative and you can change anything that is not working for you. What if every job you had was better than the last? In this reality, staying at the same job for 20 years is valuable. What if it wasn't? What if that is not true for you? For my son, the question could be: "Would you be willing to be a bad engineer and create something greater than you could imagine?"

...Just like the willingness to be a bad parent creates greater than you can imagine.

I am so grateful for my children and the amazing teenagers and young adults they are becoming. The all have this amazing ability negotiate the world with ease, to know that they know, to choose with awareness what will create more. They do not doubt who they are or their choices, which is rare in this reality. They inspire me every day. What contribution can you be and receive from your children that you have never imagined?

A question always opens the door to possibilities.

# About the Author

DR. GLENNA RICE, DPT

If you would like more ease in parenting...Glenna is a radically different wealth of possibility!

Dr. Glenna Rice, DPT (The Questionable Parent) is a single mother of three, she is also a Physical Therapist, an Access Consciousness® Certified Facilitator and an Access Body Class Facilitator. She earned her degree in Physical Therapy from the University of Southern California and worked as a Pediatric Physical Therapist in the Boston and San Francisco school districts prior to opening her own practice, Access Physical Therapy, in San Rafael, CA. She teaches "Conscious Parenting, Conscious Kids" Classes and Access Seminars for your body and life worldwide. She travels the globe teaching the Access 3 Day Body Class and the "Energetic Synthesis of Structural Embodiment" (ESSE) workshop, a hands-on course that combines the tools of Access with her years of training in manual therapy and as Physical Therapist. She is also contributing author in the book *Conscious Parents Conscious Kids* and has a monthly radio show *The Questionable Parent*. She has been using the tools of Access with her children since her youngest was one and her children have truly become a contribution to her life and living. Access has given her more ease, joy and glory with being a parent than she could have ever imagined possible?

"Being a Questionable Parent" speaks to both her willingness to continuously ask questions, and also her willingness to been seen as a less than perfect mother. She teaches parents to empower their children to know what they require and what will work for them. What if you didn't have to control who your children are? What if you could trust your awareness rather than being fearful for your children?

Since Glenna found this amazing work, every day has become a new discovery into ways to parent with more ease so it works for her and her family. She is truly creating something extraordinary with her kids. She no longer plays the insane role of mother that is normal in this reality; the role that is full of hard work, controls, over-scheduling, figuring out what is best, concern, stress and constant worry. She chooses from what is light, what is required, what will expand her life and her children's lives. She does not force her points of view on her children. She is instead an invitation to something different. She asks questions, does not look for answers and is open to infinite possibilities of how things can change and allows all the energies that are available to support her in what she is choosing to create.

Glenna sees daily the changes created in the lives of the people she works with: couples who stop hating each other, divorces that actually empower everyone involved, parents who are able to see the gifts their children with the labels of autism or ADHD truly have, mothers who create childbirth with ease, an allowance of teenagers that seemed impossible, parents having the awareness of what their children would like to be, to eat, when to sleep, eliminating so many of the struggles of parenting in this reality!

Access Consciousness may be the weirdest and wackiest system she has ever encountered...but it actually works to create the changes people are asking for! Glenna has an amazing gift to look at the energy of what you are asking to change and facilitate from that space instead of just the story. What she speaks to about parenting applies to every part of life!

Glenna's target is to facilitate as much consciousness and awareness in the lives, living and reality of everyone who is willing to choose something different and create more ease, joy and glory on this planet! What do your children know? What do you as a parent know? How can we tap into this to make a difference? Change is not always comfortable but often required. Are you willing to be the change that can truly create a difference? Are you willing to gift that to your children?

For more information on Glenna go to glennarice.com or www.drglennarice.accessconsciousness.com.

# Chapter 11

## Conscious Parenting

By Gary M. Douglas

### Parenting Is Not About Ownership and Control

Most parents think that parenting is about ownership and control. They believe they have total control of their children's life and who their children become when they grow up. The idea that parents are—or are supposed to be—in control of their children and what they do is a major misconception and leads parents to misidentify what their job is.

The truth is that parents aren't in control. It's actually the other way around. Kids are in control of themselves. Kids choose who they are going to have as parents! We don't choose them; they choose us. Children come in to this life with a point of view and a job to do. They choose us because we somehow fit in with their plan.

I was born into a family that was "normal, average, and real." In my family, we were supposed to live a normal, average life. We were not supposed to be extraordinary in any way. When I expressed interest in art, music and literature, they thought I was weird. They did nothing to encourage that, and in fact, did everything they could to discourage those interests and show me that I was wrong. They took me to lots of movies to get me to look at average stuff, cowboy movies, in particular. They wanted me to get clear that my interest in art, music and literature was leading me in the wrong direction. Of course, that didn't work. And today I am one of the weirdest, wildest, wackiest guys on the planet. It's what I chose. They could never have made me choose their way of being.

Most people have the idea that good parenting is based on being right versus being wrong. They think it's about getting "results," being in control, and having all the answers. It attempts to indoctrinate kids into a certain way of being and tries to make life predictable. The problem with trying to train kids to be normal, real, and predictable is that it imposes huge limitations and judgments on them. It does not encourage and allow for the greatness of children.

The truth is your kids are not limited, normal, average and predictable. They are magic. Their magic is their infinite being. Would you be willing to claim, own, and acknowledge that your children have magic within them?

## Are You Parenting Just Like Your Mum and Dad?

A lot of parents assume that their children are going to have a better life than they had. They try to create something different for their children than what was created for them. Often they make decisions about what was wrong with the way they were parented, and then try to create a parenting system that's different from what was given to them. Usually they go overboard in the opposite direction, which doesn't accomplish anything, except to wrap the same insanity in a slightly different package.

I remember a time I walked into the living room about two a.m. and found my oldest son watching television. I said, "Young man, don't you realize you have to get up and go to work in the morning? It's two o'clock in the morning, and you should be going to bed!"

All of a sudden, I heard my mother's words coming out of my mouth. I was speaking exactly the same words she had spoken to me when I was that age.

I realized that when I was my son's age, I wasn't any better about going to bed early than he was going to be, so I said, "Never mind. I didn't listen to my mom, and you're not going to listen to me. Good night."

I was willing to hear myself speaking as my mother and to see that I was unconsciously trying to duplicate the way she had raised me. I knew my son was not going to listen to me any more than I listened to my mom.

I was willing to ask myself, "Is it worthwhile for me to try to control this child? Or do I have to see that he's going to choose for himself, regardless of my furious attempts at control?"

When you notice yourself imposing control and limitations on your kids or trying to parent them the way you were parented, you can say, "Oops!" then destroy and uncreate whatever it was you were doing and choose again. Are you willing to give up your fixed points of view of what parenting has to look like?

## Being Aware Instead of Being Careful

Many parents make the mistake of thinking it's their job to protect their children from things that might be dangerous. They try to prevent their children from doing things that they consider dangerous. They try to keep them from doing anything that might hurt them. They try to keep them from doing things that are outside their own realm of reality. They want to make sure that nobody is going to run away with their children.

The problem with this approach is that it creates fear rather than awareness.

I didn't tell my kids not to talk to strangers. I said, "Be aware of who you're talking to." Half of the children who have been kidnapped, have been kidnapped by somebody they know. So, instead of saying, "Don't talk to strangers," it makes more sense to say, "Be aware, and if the energy doesn't feel right, get out of there. If doesn't feel right to talk to this person or if it feels yucky to you, run."

One of the greatest gifts you can give your children is an awareness of energy. They know when somebody doesn't feel right to them. You're actually keeping them much safer if you teach them to acknowledge their awareness of energies and people.

It is more important to be aware than it is to be careful. Being careful comes from the idea that everything is going to be bad and unpleasant. Being aware simply means you are attentive to the energy.

If you help your children to feel the energy of a situation and to take care of themselves by being aware, they will be able to stay out of trouble.

## Parents and Their Tendency to Be Overly Caring

I often watch mothers try to prove how much they care for their children, instead of actually caring about them. I think caring about your children is seeing them for who they are, acknowledging who they are, being grateful for who they are and not judging them for not being who you want them to be.

Most parents have misidentified and misapplied caring as controlling everything in their children's lives so the kids never make a choice that "hurts" them.

You want children to know that you care about them and that they can create their life and take care of themselves. It's important that they know they care of themselves.

You have to be willing to let your children have bad experiences. That is the hardest thing for parents to do. You can want your kids to be safe. You can want to protect your kids from having bad experiences, but you can't stop bad experiences from happening to your kids if they are not aware enough to keep bad things from happening to themselves.

When you let kids have "bad" experiences, they learn about the energy that precedes and accompanies a bad experience. They become aware and know, "Oh! When I've felt this way in the past, it was a bad experience. I'm going to choose something else."

When you help children develop their awareness of energy by allowing them to have experiences of all kinds, it helps to keep them safe for the rest of their lives.

## Honor Your Kids's Point Of View

True caring is about acknowledging the infinite choice that kids have. True caring is being willing to allow kids to make choices even if you think those choices might hurt them. Most parents think caring means something like, "I love my kids and I care about them, so I will have them do everything I've decided is best for them. I have to tell them what to do because they are too young to make decisions for themselves."

You have to be willing to take the time it takes to let your kids have their point of view and decide whether they want to change it or not. That's the most important thing you can give them—the understanding that their point of view is okay.

Most parents try to force their kids into doing what they want them to do. You have got to understand that your kids have a point of view and honor it. You can do this by asking your kids what they desire and honoring their request.

### Do I Control Them or Do I Let Them Go Wild?

When I was growing up, I did babysitting to earn money. I worked for two distinct kinds of parents. There were those who had long lists of rules their kids had to follow. These parents weren't big on communicating with their kids. They were focused on telling their kids what they could not do. The second kind of parents had a much more communicative inter-relationship with their kids. The kids of the first kind of parents, the rule makers, were the most insane to deal with. The kids of the more communicative parents were far easier to get along with and they turned out to be better people.

There are also parents who would be called "permissive." They allow their kids to do whatever they wanted to do, without ever communicating or sharing with them an awareness of what can occur. These parents follow behind their kids, picking up their messes and taking care of them. They don't want to have confrontations with their children. This is not what I am referring to when I talk about communicative parents.

Communicative parents communicate with their kids all the time. They are present with their kids energetically and they acknowledge who their kids are. They're not saying, "Oh, go do what you want in the world. I'm not going to be here when you get back."

It's more like, "How did your day go today? What did you learn? What is showing up?" You are communicating with them; you're not trying to control them. Communication is the key.

However, there are some places where a little control is helpful. When my kids were really little, I'd say, "Okay, let's clean up your room," and they would say, "No. I don't want to!"

I would take their little hands and together we would pick each thing up and put it in the toy box. I wouldn't clean their room up for them. I had them do it. This was more work than doing it myself, but after a short period of time, when I would say, "It's time to clean up your room now," they would clean it up. It's a different way of doing things. They learned that they could clean up their room when they had to.

I am talking about becoming aware of what is required of you to be with your children in each moment. It is not about control or no control. Many parents often want to do either/ or. "Do I control them or do I let them go wild?" Neither. Parenting is not an either/or proposition. That, once again, is looking for an answer to for everything. You want to get the answer right so that everything is taken care of forever and you don't have to be aware anymore. True parenting— conscious parenting—involves awareness. It's not about getting one answer and one rule and then enforcing it forever. It's being aware of where your children are all the time, how they're functioning and what's going on.

### Encourage Awareness Rather Than Making Rules

I take the approach of asking kids to be aware—not giving them rules. When my kids were little, I would say, "If you touch that stove, it's going to be hot." I wouldn't say, "No, don't touch the stove."

Ultimately "no" becomes a place where you have to be in control of the kid, instead of inviting them being in control of themselves. "If you touch that stove, it's going to be hot," is information and encourages awareness, rather than, "Don't touch it." My kids would feel the heat of the stove and would know not to touch it. There is, of course, always one child who has to test everything, but most of the time, if you give kids information instead of rules, it's amazing what will happen.

When you treat your kids as though they know what you're saying, they know what you're saying. Sometimes they may not understand the words, but you can give them pictures of what will happen. Sometimes you communicate with them telepathically.

These things are possible and yet many parents will not allow these possibilities into their awareness. Can you imagine how many possibilities parents cut out of their awareness when they buy into the limited perspective of conventional parenting?

## I Live with My Kids Moment by Moment

There is a lot of psychobabble about positive parenting. Like if you see your children as wonderful, then you create the space for them to go into being wonderful; if you see your children as horrible brats, then you create the space for that. It's like "The Secret" of parenting—what you focus on is what you get.

From my point of view, it's preferable not to focus on anything. I live with my kids moment by moment. This is a bizarre idea for many parents, but ultimately it works. To do this, you have to take each event separately. People try to create a system by which they govern their parenting so they are always consistent. But are any two days the same? No. Do any two kids react the same? No. Does your child react the same way every day? No. Do you ever act the same way two days in a row? Or do you change all the time? And when somebody tries to put you in a place where they expect you to respond the same way twice in a row, do you resist and react to that?

When you have a fixed point of view or an expectation about how your children should behave and act, how much freedom does it give them? It doesn't give them any, because your expectation defines their choice. If parents put their point of view on their kids—"John's going to react this way" or "Suzy's going to react that way"—they limit the kids' choices.

When parents have expectations, kids have to align and agree with their parents' expectations and do what they're expected to do, or they have to resist and react to the expectations and do the opposite. The children don't have the freedom to be who they are in that 10 seconds. Ultimately, isn't what you want for your children for them to be who they are, regardless of whether you agree with it or not?

It's important to acknowledge what kids know and what they are aware of, even when they're very young. They are infinite beings—even if their bodies are small.

# About the Author

GARY DOUGLAS

Best-selling author, international speaker and a sought-after facilitator, Gary Douglas is known for his intensity of awareness and his incredible capacity to facilitate people to *"know what they know."* He chooses to embody consciousness in everything that he does which inspires others to choose to become more conscious as a result.

Gary came with an exceptional level of awareness into the Midwest middle class "white bread" family and lived the *Leave it to Beaver* childhood. He has a very different view on life and realized that he was so different from most of the people he knew, when he was only six years old. He became aware of this difference by watching people create their lives and seeing that none of it was about the joy and the possibilities—it was always about the wrongness of everything. Gary knew there had to be more than this reality was offering since there was nothing about it that was magical, joyful or expansive. So, he began seeking deeper awareness to life's mysteries at an early age. Along the way he uncovered a new way forward—one that would create change in the world and in people's lives. He discovered that magic is all around us; it's something we create—its consciousness. He recognized that the capacity to be more aware and more conscious was every person's gift if they were willing to choose it.

Over time what he recognized as the gift he was, was his intensity of awareness and his capacity to invite people to consciousness and to recognize that everything is possible and nothing is impossible. His gift is his ability to look at life, the universe and the consciousness that we all are, as well as the possibilities that are an intrinsic part of it from a space that no one else has ever chosen.

## Empowering people to see different possibilities

Gary has become an internationally recognized thought leader in transforming lives and creating different choices— willing to empower people to see different possibilities and to recognize what is truly possible for them. Gary is acknowledged worldwide for his unique perspectives on personal transformation that are unlike anything else in the world. He is not aligned with any particular religion or tradition. Through his writing and workshops, he gifts processes and tools that bring within reach the ease, joy and glory of life, and the magic of happiness that expand into more awareness, joy and abundance. His simple yet profound teachings have already facilitated countless people throughout the world to "know what they know" and to realize what they can choose that they never realized they could choose.

## At the core of his teachings lies the transformation of consciousness

After recognizing that greater consciousness in people can change the direction of their lives and the future of the planet, the creation and expansion of Access Consciousness® by

Gary has been primarily driven by a single question: "What can I do to help the world?"

He continues to inspire others, inviting the awareness of a different possibility across the world and making an immense contribution to the planet. He facilitates people to know that they are the source for creating the change they desire and creating a life that goes beyond the limitations of what the rest of the world thinks is important. He sees this as an essential aspect to creating a future that has greater possibilities in it for everyone as well as the planet. This is a priority not only for personal happiness but also for the ending of violent conflict endemic on our planet and creating a different world. If enough people choose to be more aware and more conscious, they will start to see the possibilities of what they have available to them and change what is occurring here on planet earth.

## Author

Gary Douglass is the author of the bestselling novel, *The Place*. This book is about people knowing that all things are possible and choice is the source of creation. Gary is also the co-author of a variety of books on the subjects of money, relationships, magic and animals with internationally renowned Energy Transformation virtuoso Dr Dain Heer.

## Inspiring people worldwide

Gary pioneered a set of transformational life changing tools and processes known as Access Consciousness® over 20 years ago. These leading edge tools have transformed the lives of thousands of people all over the world. His work has spread to 173 countries, with over 2,000 trained facilitators worldwide. Simple but so effective, the tools facilitate people of all ages and backgrounds to help remove limitations holding them back from a full life.

# Chapter 12

## What Is a Mother?

By Fay Thompson

I always said I never wanted kids. I always knew I would have them. Five years into my marriage, I agreed to be open to having a child. I was pregnant within a month.

I remember the day I took the pregnancy test. I knew I should be happy and overjoyed. I knew I should feel amazing. I did not feel those things. Instead, I felt like something inside me broke. I felt some heavy thing drop from my heart and hit my stomach with a deep thud. I didn't know what it was at the time, but something changed inside me that day.

When I told my husband the news of the pregnancy, he was elated. His joy somehow made me feel worse. It made me feel wrong for experiencing what I was experiencing. I didn't have any of the "glowing" people talk about when they refer to pregnant women. I had morning sickness for the first five months and felt fat, ugly, and uncomfortable for the final four.

That I could handle. The worst part was I didn't feel like me anymore.

I felt like I was failing pregnancy, but I wasn't. I had a beautiful, healthy, baby girl inside of me. When she was born, I felt a love for her that I didn't know I could feel. I had never seen anything so beautiful in my whole life. I adored my child, but still something wasn't quite right with me. I still felt frustration, resentment, fear, and anger for being tied down with a child.

The next year I had another beautiful baby girl. I had accepted my fate of being a mother and was doing my best to make sure they were cared for and loved.

Fast forward about 10 years. I still had two beautiful, healthy girls. I still had a husband who was overjoyed by them. And then there was me. I still felt trapped. I still felt resentment; not all the time, but it was there. As embarrassed as I am to admit, I sometimes wondered what my life would have been like if I hadn't become a mother.

I was so conflicted by it all. I had such an intense desire to have the freedom of not having children in my life so that I could create my life without worry of how it might affect them. I also love my kids the way any parent loves their children. It is inexplicable, but if you are a parent, I suspect you know what I am talking about. I would never get rid of, give away, or run away from my children, ever. I would be crushed in a way I can't describe if anything harmful ever happened to them. They bring a happiness to me that I could not know if they hadn't been born.

There was so much I wanted to do and create, but felt I didn't have the money, or the time, or the freedom, or the luxury. I felt it would be selfish. I had a business I desperately wanted to grow, but felt held back from doing that because I was a mother.

For the longest time, I thought I was crazy, and a horrible mother, and a horrible person. Then I talked to some other mothers who felt the same way as I did and had the same experiences that I had. This begged the question: Could I be a parent and be free at the same time?

There was both a lightness and a heaviness around this question for me. I knew it meant there was a truth with a lie attached to it, that some part of this was true while another part was not. When I asked what part was the lie, I realized it was what I thought a mother was, and who I had to be in order to be one. As I explored the energies presented to me by this question, the same heaviness that I felt the moment I found out I was pregnant kept coming back to me. I decided to go explore that moment to find out exactly what the heaviness was.

As I sat with it and asked questions around it, I came to the realization that the moment I found out I was pregnant, I stopped being me and instead became "a mother." Instead of seeing my forthcoming child as a contribution that added to me and my life, I allowed pregnancy to replace me and my life with the title and life of "a mother." I believe this is what my mother did and perhaps what the mothers before her did. We gave up our lives in order to have children.

This was a huge epiphany. I had stopped being me the moment I found out I was pregnant and truly thought I had no other choice. In that moment, I decided that since I was now a mother I had to live out all the definitions, expectations, and projections of whatever that meant.

Furthermore, I knew what the definition of a mother was to me and it had nothing to do with me, the being, the person inside who loved fun, freedom, playfulness, and whimsy. While one would think having children would be a perfect fit for someone who likes these things, my definition of a mother did not allow for any of it. In my world, a mother was someone who was responsible and took care of things. She was the problem solver, the teacher, and the disciplinarian. A mother told you what to do and not do. A mother was the one who taught you right from wrong. A mother was safe and dependable. A mother was always there when you needed her. A mother was an example of morality for her children and the pillar of righteousness.

No wonder I felt the way I did. I can't imagine a life more boring, more judgmental, and more anti-fun. I had bought into it; I was living it; and I was miserable.

I went back, in my mind, to the moment when I found out that I was pregnant and I talked to myself at that time. I told her this news didn't have to mean what she thought it meant, and she didn't have to decide what her mother and the mothers before her had decided. I let her know she could still be her even if she had children, and that those children could be a major contribution to her if she would let them. I let her know she didn't have to give up her dreams and she never had to be somebody else just because she might be pregnant. I asked her to ponder what she wished she could have had from her parents that she never got, and asked her if she was able and willing to provide that for her children if she had them. I let her know that every definition, expectation, and projection of what a mother is was just a made up construct and that she could choose anything outside of those definitions, expectations, and projections that made life fun for her. I gave myself permission to no longer be a mother, but instead be me with children who added to my wonderful life. When I relived the moment of finding out I was pregnant, I no longer felt broken and I no longer felt the heavy weight in my chest or stomach. Instead, I felt a light growing in my heart and space being created for me and my unborn child. I actually sensed that this could be a lot of fun. Until then, I had never known that was possible.

This was a game changer. I felt totally different about my life, my business, my children, my husband, and about myself. Shortly after I made this discovery, I made the decision to take my children to a class in New York City over a long weekend. We had so much fun together going to a Broadway Show, being mesmerized by the lights and crowds in Times Square, visiting the biggest toy store I had ever been to, and taking a tour of Central Park. My children loved it all. I even took us to The Metropolitan Museum of Art! It was far more fun for me than them, but I had provided enough fun for them on the trip, they were willing to indulge me.

If I hadn't changed my mind about being a mother, I never would have taken them to New York or to the class we attended. I would have seen it as too much work and too much of a burden. I would have had many excuses about why it would not be safe for them to be there or that it would cost too much for them to go. Instead, the whole trip was fun and engaging. We made wonderful memories and created some very happy moments on that trip. Ironically, the class we attended was all about being yourself in front of others and finding your voice. We all benefitted from it.

I know this book is about parenting, and while I haven't talked much about the act of parenting, I have found that by redefining my definition of what a parent and, more specifically, what a mother is, has helped me be a better and happier person. I have happier children who no longer feel like a burden to me. I no longer feel trapped by my circumstances. I actually sense the contribution they are to my life, my business, my marriage, and me. I couldn't even begin to see that before.

By truly being ourselves, no matter how far off from the

definition of mother, father, or parent that is, we can only be a contribution to our children. By being ourselves, we teach our children to be themselves. Perhaps that is the true definition of a parent: to allow your children to be themselves while being yourself. I wonder what life might be like if we all had that while growing up?

If you are a mother or father who has felt the way I did, please know you are not wrong, weird, or worrisome. You just likely gave yourself up to be a parent. If you aren't sure, just ask, "Did I give myself up in order to become a mother/father/parent?" or "Now that I am a parent, do I no longer get to be me?" You might wish to go back to the moment where you made that decision and talk to yourself at that time. Let that younger you know s/he doesn't have to make that decision and other options are available, including the one to continue being you while allowing the child to be a contribution to your life and living.

If you love your child enough to give yourself up for them, could you love them and you enough to *be yourself* for them? Would you be willing to destroy every definition of mother/father/parent that you have that doesn't allow you to be you?

As a funny anecdote, after I allowed myself to be me again, I realized that I actually did want children. I just never wanted be a mother, because of what I thought that meant I had to become.

# About the Author

FAY THOMPSON

Fay Thompson. B.Ed., is an Access Consciousness® Certified Facilitator and Licensed Spiritual Health Coach who specializes in Subconscious Mind Correction. She is also a spiritual facilitator and lecturer who offers private intuitive sessions and various workshops. Her aim is to empower each person to live from a place of truth and realize the immense potential within. Her work has been featured in various publications and on CBC Radio and CBC TV. Her first book, *Azez Medicine: Healing the Mind, Body, and Spirit with the Help of The Beings of the Light*, reached #1 on Amazon's New Releases List and established Fay as an expert in spiritual development. Fay lives in Saskatchewan, Canada with her wonderful husband and two amazing daughters who keep her grounded and laughing. For more information on Fay and her work, visit www.faythompson.com or find her on Facebook at www.facebook.com/faythompson8.

# Chapter 13

## Stepping Out of Judgment

By Susan Lazar Hart

First off, thank you for stopping by this chapter.

Whether you are a parent or a child... whether you have ever been, or will ever become either of those, this chapter may hold some keys to a freedom you may not have known was possible for being in a family.

How many of us have held ourselves hostage, imprisoned by self-criticism and judgment because we or someone else concluded we had done a terrible job at parenting? We wait for validation from someone else to set us free, when the only one who can really set you free you is you. The freedom you seek lies in your willingness to let go of what you are using to hold yourself back—judgment.

Would you be willing to be more of you than you have ever been?

How many of us were taught from a very young age that there was something about us that we had to fix, to make better, to apologize for? Could those be major judgments we bought from our parents, teachers or peers?

What if the purpose and target of judgment was to keep you from being you?

Who did we all buy that from anyway? What if I told you that everything you have ever punished yourself with, all those criticisms you have held onto all these years as a wrongness about you, and every thought that is limiting you, is not yours at all.

What if everything you've believed was a wrongness was actually a strongness?

You see, someone has to create the initial judgment for you to buy. It is not real. You can't hold it in your hand or purchase it at the store. When you walk into a forest, do you hear the trees judging each other for the quality of their leaves? Does a bird stop singing when it hears another bird singing louder, softer, or differently?

It's more like a broken telephone where the original perpetrator judges him/herself and then deflects that new configuration on to someone else until it reaches you. What if judgment was someone else's way of holding you back from greatness? Remember this: judgment it is not real. Believe it, and you begin to create the limitation keeping you from everything that is possible

Did you know that we are the only creatures on the planet that create judgment, defending ourselves by the rightness or wrongness of it, holding ourselves hostage?

The greatest gift you can give your kids is to step out of being a victim and step into being you. I am not saying they will like it. I am not saying it won't be uncomfortable. Are you willing to be true to you and what you desire? No matter what it looks like? No matter what it takes? Or would you rather buy more judgment from others?

What I know for sure is that we have a choice. There have been many moments in the deep, dark hours of night when I have found myself wandering through doubt, wondering if I might have done more harm than good. And the bottom line is that it takes courage to get off the see-saw of good and bad, right and wrong. Stepping out of self-judgment requires courage and creativity. It requires taking a deep breath and facing your worst fears—that you may be the worst parent that ever lived. The truth is, as much as we fly on the wings of our children's successes, we also crawl through the blood, sweat and the tears of their tough lessons. When we take on our children's lives as ours, when we judge anything as a "lesson," we lose the sense of adventure, the sense of possibility. Whatever you judge kills any gratitude or peace that would otherwise be available, no matter whose family or what relationship you are in.

And ultimately it is about you, your growth and your discovering the magic that only you know is true for you along the way.

Rick and I have been together for 40 years. We have a blended family with four grown up children, their three partners, a very young grand being and another on the way.

I became a parent at the age of 21 when I got together with Rick, a widower with two young boys. I realize now how much I was mimicking the way I was parented, all-the-time knowing it was not working for anyone. I remembered hoping no one could see what a disaster of a parent I had become. As one of my sons told me later, I really became a mother when I gave birth to the girls.

And so I stopped trying to control everyone and everything: the punishments, the yelling, the over-drinking; and I began to listen, really listen, to these incredible beings and to what I knew was possible for all of us, and most of all, for me.

I remember when one of my daughters became a juvenile

diabetic at age 14. I came to realize that her body was hers and it was her choice and not mine to choose what and how to deal with the situation.

Rick and I gave her the space and freedom to work out how to navigate it. The people around us—the other parents—were upset I wasn't researching it. The "other" people around us wanted me to make sure I was on top of everything. I looked at how she was handling it and without skipping a beat, thought to myself, "This is hers; my job is to be a mother, without judgment." This was her journey; to figure out how she was going to be with it and work with diabetes for the rest of her life, not mine.

So many parents take over their kids' lives. They step in and take over their teens' lives. This basically devastates any possibility for the child to be self-sufficient and resilient.

What if there was no such thing as failure?

What if each day was its very own day, and the success was living each day to the fullest? We build hysteria by choosing to be in judgment of our children. What if there was a different way of being?

How many people have the courage to step out of what is expected of or projected on them? You have to be willing to do this in order to have the freedom to be you as a parent.

And this is just as true with our relationships with adult children. All of my four children are adults now. All of them have totally different relationships with me and with their dad. We are different; we as parents are changing daily. So are they. We all have our own lives. Some of them I hear from daily, some not at all. None of it is significant. It's just a choice. Would you be willing not to define yourself by what this reality says a "good family" should look like?

What if you could let that go? How much have we all been taught to create "connection points" or some false commonality with which we anchor to each other and call that "relationship"? What if we could create much more generative relationships with our children by simply asking, "What would you like me to be for you?" rather than insisting that we hash out the problems? How often do people create problems with their children to make sure they are needed? They struggle to be in touch with them constantly, to know what's going on in their lives because this somehow validates their own. How many people hold onto a problem to show they are concerned, to prove they care or have something in common? That's what I call creating a false sense of intimacy.

They chose you for a reason. What if you could create your relationship as something fun, something that's a contribution to both of your lives, rather than the trauma and drama most people create parent-child relationships from?

I have a close relationship with some of my children. Some I may speak to daily, some not at all. Some I speak to many times per day. We share the little things, like showing off a new pair of shoes, talking about our work. With every child, when I reach out, I reach out to what they can hear. Nothing is required in return. The gift is in the willingness to be without judgment.

Who could you be if you stopped looking for connection points and started creating what you came here to be?

When you start to change the way you relate within the family, you start to change the way you relate to your life, your body, your living, yourself, your money flows. You start to change how you relate to everything in your life.

How many children subjugate themselves for their parents? How many parents subjugate themselves for their children? No one really ever stops to ask, "What is this creating?"

What if that is one of the biggest lies of this reality? Parents are saying they give up everything for their children;

and children are making choices to please their parents. What would be different if we all let this go? If we gave up giving ourselves up?

When you give up defending what you have given up, or have decided you had to give up, this gives your children the space to step into true choice for themselves as well, without judgment, without the need for your approval or requirement of your allowance.

This is a different dance, one with no followers. And it could be the most uncomfortable choice you have ever made.

As a teen, I would often come home late at night and find my mom sitting in the living room in the dark, the red embers of her cigarette glowing from one hand, a cognac in the other as she sang to Peggy Lee's song: "Is That All There Is? If that's all there is my friends, then let's keep dancing. Lets break out the booze and have a ball if that's all there is." Mom was brilliant. She wrote poems. She ran a business. In her youth, she had wanted to be in the theater, but her family forbade her. "Only whores are in the theater," they told her. That was in 1930. For most of her life, she could not see her own gifts. She was dynamic and vibrant and could belly up to the bar with the best of them. Her constant self-judgment was the thread of depression that wove through her life as she constantly asked, "Is That All There Is?"

How many people live lives of quiet desperation, in judgment of themselves? How many parents look to their children as a reflection of their value?

Stepping out of judgment of myself was the key that changed everything for me. For years, I had this horror of how I viewed myself as a parent. What if someone found out? What if I was the most horrible person that ever was?

I saw my life as a deep dark secret. No one can judge you as much as you judge you—that is the quiet life of desperation

Henry Walden Thoreau speaks so well of. No one can judge you as much as you judge yourself.

So what about you?

Would you be willing to release every judgment you have of yourself as a parent?

Would you be willing to be in allowance of everything you have created, and every choice you've ever made?

When I was younger, traveling the world, I got a job working in Norway at an apple farm. One night while at dinner, the farmer knocked over a glass of milk spilling it everywhere. My entire body contracted. I was ready for an angry outburst! At my house, where I grew up, that would have led to screaming and name calling. Instead, everyone burst out laughing. This was such a different way of being, it completely opened up my world. What if no one was wrong, ever? How many people look to match the vibration of wrongness they grew up with, then pass it on to their children as if it were real or true? Remember, wrongness is always a judgment and every judgment is a creation... a creation that someone along the way probably invented to keep you from shining as brightly, from shining *brighter*, than them.

The truth is that every moment you are judging you, you are transferring that judgment to your child, no matter what age they are. Sometimes I feel parenting is really about the willingness to acknowledge what is, find the humor in it, no matter what it looks like, no matter what it takes. Change happens in a moment, when a breakthrough happens.

This is your life. This is what it takes. Step out of judgment. How many of you have decided that if you are not happy in your intimate relationships with your children, you will not be happy? Years ago, I looked in the mirror and I asked myself, "Is this what you want to be doing with your life? Look at your life-is what you are being now creating the the future you have been asking for?"

And so I began to choose differently, to choose that which would create something greater.

This is your life, not your children's life. You must choose for you... and be in allowance of what they are choosing for themselves. What I know for sure is that every one of my four children is a gift to me. They each have come to me and been my teacher in different ways. Yes, it was not always comfortable. Sometimes it was hell, sometimes it was heaven, and all of it was within my creation.

Remember; this is your life, not your children's life.

As promised at the beginning, I have introduced several questions I use as keys that open up a window of possibilities. Please feel free to use one or all of these keys as you continue to discover a path to a freedom you may not have ever known was possible, family or no family.

Each key, when practiced daily, is one which may open the door to a myriad of possibilities for something greater to show up and perhaps even change your life.

1. Cultivate intimacy with yourself.

True intimacy is the willingness to honor yourself with what you choose, to trust that you know, to be in allowance for whatever shows up, to be vulnerable with whatever you choose and the willingness to be grateful for you and who you are choosing to be

2. Spend some time discovering you. Gift yourself an hour a day and one day a week to pamper you and indulge your desires.

3. Stack the good and savor it.

Ask yourself every evening, "What am I grateful for today?"

Keep a gratitude journal

4. When you find yourself buried under a relationship with your children or a parent, with a spouse or a partner, take a deep breath and take one step today that will change your life in every way.

Begin by asking a question. Ask, "Who am I being?" and "Who am I being this for?"

Then let it go

Every time you find yourself judging you, stop and ask, "Who does this judgment belong to?" And let that go. Chances are, none of that judgment was yours to begin with!

What are you walking away with after reading this chapter? What keys have worked for you? What questions do you have?

I would love to hear from you. You can contact me anytime at info@rightrelationshipforyou.com.

# About the Author

SUSAN LAZAR HART

Susan Lazar Hart travels the world as a "Conscious Thought" leader, radio host, motivational speaker and as the Executive Director of Right Relationship For You™.

Susan combines the tools of Access Consciousness® with her real world experience as a wife, mother, life coach and relationship counselor to introduce people to a whole new possibility in their relationships to themselves. Whether you're sorting out issues with your partner, your children, your boss, your body or even your finances... Susan Lazar Hart delivers information that is easy to understand and gets results.

A favorite at women's conferences and Natural Living Expos in Canada and the United States, Susan Lazar Hart is a crowd pleaser as an invitation to intimacy and relationships from a different point of view. Her straight-forward approach and irreverent sense of humor keeps audiences mesmerized as she shares tools that are not only simple to use, they get immediate and profound results. Put simply, Susan is transforming the way people around the world view themselves.

Here are some comments from a recent class:

*Thank you Susan! Thank you for being in my life! It's been now a couple days of total lightness! I have not experienced anything like this for... mmm... I actually don't remember when I had such experience...*
GP - Montreal

*Susan is the key Right Relationship facilitator... tremendously caring as well as fun.*
DL – Australia

"Intimacy and Relationships, like gardens, must begin with seeds that are nurtured, cared for and cultivated with awareness."

Susan Lazar Hart is an invitation to intimacy and relationships from a different point of view. Her classes and talks are for singles or couples of all orientations, lengths of commitment, and stages of life.

Email: info@susanlazarhart.com

Website: www.rightrelationshipforyou.com

# Chapter 14

## The Choice of Happiness; Teens Done Different

By Julie Oreson Perkins,
with her teens Connor and Christy

Greetings from Boulder, Colorado, USA where I live with my husband, two wonderful teenagers and one orange tabby cat. Our dream house backs up to open space with views of the mountains. We have satisfying jobs that pay the bills, friends, and "renewed" health (especially since I am a breast cancer survivor!). We have been active in our communities and our kids' lives (schools, hobbies, Scouting, sports), and we are happy. "Life is good" as the saying goes... right?

Yes! And it hasn't always been easy. Sure, the early years were total ease. I was the first of my friends to quit a secure government job to start a "home-based" business and hire nannies for the kids. I managed my business and the household by blending what worked for us, with the "best practices" of society and business at that time.

When the kids started going to preschool, I started to really see how what we were doing was different. I would share with other parents what we were choosing and how well it worked for us. The response was sometimes admiration, but more often judgment about how "unusual" we were. About that same time, I observed just how "different" our kids were, too—smart and amazingly intuitive. While we as parents were proud of that, it also worried us since we didn't want them to be singled out because of that difference. I would ask, "Are you sure you want to wear that outfit to school today?" in an attempt to shield them from becoming a target. The answer was often, "Yeah, mom. It's OK. I'm the weird kid and everybody knows it."

Instead of believing or trusting them, I embarked on a campaign to teach my kids how to "fit in" and "be the same" as everyone else. When things weren't working at school, I demanded that the teachers or parents "make this right" so that my kids wouldn't be excluded. When the schools didn't (couldn't!) manage or change the situations, I asked the kids what they desired, also offering to change schools... which we did—a lot. Those choices afforded them (and me) some semblance of "empowerment," —plus occasional, yet temporary, "pockets" of happiness.

In the middle school years, we really began noticing how hard things had become. The kids were starting to "swim in bigger ponds" and the water wasn't always as clear there. There were "rules" and so-called "choice" (as long as you chose the school's way), most of which wasn't working for my out-of-the-box kids who tended to speak up and say what was true for them. Tired, cranky and frustrated from always standing up for my kids, I downshifted into blaming the schools and yelling at my kids to "be more normal" so as not to "rock the boat."

That's when I started to get that all of these things and people (schools, teachers, peers, coaches, leaders, etc) were not going to change, and that something in *us* needed to change. Yet, by this time my kids had soaked up so much about how things had to be in school—and about how I said they should "fit in" to avoid judgment—that they were drowning in opinions that weren't even theirs.

As a parent, I was drowning too, from feeling like a failure for not protecting my kids from this "cruel and unkind world" and all the things that people were doing that I had decided were "insane." I was "sick and tired" (literally! I became a cancer patient!) and I began seeking different healing modalities in the hopes of changing this "drowning effect" for me—and possibly for my kids too. Nothing seemed to work for me until I learned the different and practical tools and techniques of Access Consciousness®. As I took classes, I got a better sense of my part in creating all this mess, which is when things started to change quickly and easily for me— and that change rippled out through the family. The kids have been taking more Access classes recently too (one of the gifts of Access is that kids can attend also!) and changing dynamically as a result. Our favorite tool is that we all have total choice—especially now that we know that Choice Creates and that Happiness is Just a Choice!

Our son Connor is doing things differently. After enrolling in an online school for his senior year—and graduating there instead of the local high school—he attended a local university for almost a year. He's now choosing to work full-time instead of going back to college like his peers. He has also chosen to live with friends instead of at home—friends who "get him" and "have his back" instead of those who judge or use him. He's getting clearer on what works for him and what makes him happy! I had the rare opportunity to talk for hours with him about this on a recent drive from Colorado to California. We drove through many beautiful landscapes, including the desert. In such beautiful nature spaces, we both felt more at peace and ease, which allowed us to see each other from a different perspective—and acknowledge who and where we both are now, no matter what choices we are currently making. We dove deep into topics like relationships, sex, drugs, legalized marijuana, alcohol, money and what it takes to be ourselves. I asked him questions like, "What would you tell other teens about being who they truly are? And about being happy?" I love his clear and simple insights:

**Connor**:

• Everybody marches to the beat of their own drum. So, what's right for somebody else may not be right for you. And that's OK.

• Don't ever dis-honor yourself by trying to make yourself like someone else—especially if you know that isn't working for you.

• And never dis-service somebody else by trying to make them like you because that's just as detrimental to them as it is to you.

Our daughter Christy is also choosing differently. She is pursuing her dream of becoming a singer/songwriter at a boarding arts high school atop a mountain in California, surrounded by nature. When I asked her about happiness and how she chose it, this is what she wrote:

**Christy**: The simple truth is that real happiness can never come from anybody but you. You have to be totally willing to be happy and choose that—regardless of WHATEVER is happening in your world or WHOEVER is around you.

I was looking for the "key to happiness" when Dr. Dain Heer, co-creator of Access Consciousness asked me, "Are you willing to be happy? Even if you're the only one?" My mind couldn't even process this. Then I realized why—because if I were happy, then I'd be alone since none of my friends were happy. Like them, I was listening to the media tell me how to "fix" my (awful) body—or how much prettier I'd be with the newest line of makeup or clothing. I was surrounded by people who bought, and re-sold, lies like that and more. As a musician and student, I was constantly being pushed to be something that I "should" be. I was never happy because the world I lived in wasn't happy—and I was just imitating that.

For so long, sadness and "depression" was comfortable for me. Since it was all around me, I didn't really see any other options. **My entire life became a cycle of longing for happiness yet thinking that I didn't deserve it—and then falling back into being depressed**. It felt easier to choose the sadness. So I did, and I thought that was working for me. Looking back, it was the most destructive thing I ever did to myself. It took destroying my mind, my relationships and my friendships—plus cutting my physical body—to realize just what that constant cycle had done to me. Yet at that point, I felt I was in too deep to even dare think about happiness— because I *really* didn't deserve it now because of what I had been doing to myself. I was just recreating this over and over again to stay in what I had decided was comfortable. I became an exhausting person to be around because I didn't want to change or be happy (even though I sometimes said I did)— and the constant flip flopping was draining me and everyone around me.

My parents especially were noticing my dramatic changes. I had become so uncomfortable in my own skin that I felt completely ok with harming it on a regular basis. I was always defensive and moody, weak and tired, hidden and unhappy, and wearing heavy, long-sleeved clothing in 100-degree heat.

They were so confused. They didn't know how to handle my situation and I truly don't blame them. It got to the point where my mother demanded to see my wrists and legs. I was regretful and exposed, and I didn't feel comfortable, even around her. I was given two options: see a therapist and tell my dad what I was doing to myself... or go to the hospital. I chose the option of therapy and letting my secret out. The next day I woke up and went through what became daily, routine check of my wrists, stomach and thighs. My mom told me that both her and my dad just wanted to help me; yet I was still so uneasy about the whole situation. Three therapists and a whole lot of meltdowns later, I was **still** uneasy. It took me years to realize that I was so unhappy because I never got to really choose. I didn't get to choose something different myself; I felt limited to the options that were thrown at me.

It's important to say this now: My parents were not wrong for what they did to try and help me from their point of view... and I wasn't wrong for what I did to myself to get to that point either. And yet, I wonder what it would have been like if I was asked (or if I had even asked myself!) this question: "What would contribute to you (or me) the most *right now*?" I started asking that and sometimes the answer was a therapy appointment. Other times it was getting different support from my family (like getting them to ask me that question), or getting outside in nature more, or talking with someone different.

I realize now that you will never really know what's going on inside the other person's head if that person doesn't want you to know. (I became really good at hiding things.) So ask that question—a lot—even if the possible answers seem too damn scary to hear. Teens know what they need, even if they're not able to say so in that exact moment. Chances are that they feel exposed, upset and *alone* like I did. Acting surprised or upset won't help... what will help is staying calm and simply letting your teen know that they're not alone. And that they can choose whatever they want. I get that this isn't easy for parents to stay calm. Be calm anyway.

Here's another important thing: *allowance.* Trusting that your child is going to choose what they will, when they will, despite all your parenting. Allowing both their and your choices to be heard will set you both free. As distressing as this is to parents of someone who is cutting, being in allowance will make both your lives easier if the act is acknowledged as a choice... if it is not judged... if neither of you make yourself wrong in the situation. The cool thing about choice is that it's only "good for 10 seconds" as they say in Access. You can choose again—and again. Parents, if you give your teens the option to choose for themselves about everything—including cutting—in most cases, they will eventually feel the freedom to choose something new or different or beyond the cutting, like I did. Plus, you won't be exhausting yourself by constantly trying to follow them around to save or rescue them.

**Julie**: Christy asked me to chime in here about "saving" and "rescuing" which was one of my big, former, self-assigned parental job duties. I say "former" because I don't do that anymore for two reasons.

Reason #1: It's disempowering—especially to the kids. How? Simply put, when you swoop in to rescue, it's basically saying that they can't handle it, and because of that, you're going to do so for them. From my perspective, it's egoic and taking a superior stance. Plus it's also a big lie; the lie being that they don't know what to do or how to do it. They DO. We ALL really KNOW what's going on if we are functioning from our "knowing."

Asking simple questions like, "What's going on here?" and "What do you (or I) know about that?" or "What could you (or

I) choose now that would change everything?" will draw out what is truly known about the situation from both sides—and empower them (and you!) to continue following the path of awareness.

Reason #2: "Saving" doesn't work because the person you "save" isn't choosing it. You are choosing it for them. Plus it consumes large amounts of everyone's time, energy and attention. That had become a pattern for us. As the "household manager" it was my job to "oversee" all things kid-related. So, that meant "fixing" anything that was "out of order" with how things are "supposed" to be... especially something deemed "dark" and "horrible" by this reality like cutting. Once I took a step back, took a few deep breaths, and really opened up my eyes to see what was there, I got that it was a choice. Even if her choices led to her leaving her body now as a "young teen" (another devastating and "unthinkable" thing in this reality).

I still got the concept that "choice creates." Interestingly enough, my choice to be the observer (instead of the "manager") of her choices allowed her more space to maneuver around any obstacles to her choosing differently. What was especially freeing for me was to acknowledge aloud to her that, "I see and allow your choices, including if you choose to leave now. I would still love you and miss you—and I know that it's still your choice." I distinctly remembering the sensation that I perceived for both of us after that conversation. It literally felt like we had been "unshackled" from something, and from each other.

**Christy**: It took me until recently to choose being the "only happy person" in my life. I wasn't willing to let the toxic people in my life go. I wasn't willing choose something so new and different because I was so comfortable with sadness. At some point I realized how much this was ruining me and keeping me in that same dark place. I finally said, "ENOUGH!"

*I finally chose for myself.* I stopped hanging out with the people who were in the same position as I was—especially since they weren't willing to change and I now was. I stopped trying to save them, which only put me back into the same cycle. When my mom stopped trying to save me, it showed me that I could choose that also with those people.

Then I finally chose to throw away the razor blades, enjoy new people, get out of the house more, and slowly step into life. The seemingly smallest things can help, like taking a walk around the neighborhood.

What would I say to other teens and parents who are where we were? **Please know and trust that you have the power to change this, if you choose**. Even if it seems like there's not a single thing to like about life—or yourself—please take a closer look. There will always be at least one thing. I knew people who looked in the mirror and gagged at their own reflection, yet they absolutely adored their eyes, hair, or other things like their fashion sense, the music they listened to or the art they created. There was a point where I was so miserable that I could barely move... but I still loved to create music and art. The "way out" of this is to find your own thing. Appreciate it. Build off it as a first step. And dream again. Even if any of this is impossible to see, it's worth prying your eyes open to look at it. It all starts with the *willingness* to be the only happy person in the room, in the city, in the country, in the whole freakin' world, if that's what it takes! **Are you willing to be totally and truly happy? No matter what?!**

**Final words from Julie:** Connor, Christy and I genuinely hope that both teens and parents will get something out of reading this. When working with my life-coaching clients who are parents of teens, I am often asked to share my top three tips. So here goes:

1. **Change the environment** to get a different perspective. My kids and I have always loved being out in nature, so we go there for quicker shift and change!

2. **Ask questions** (LOTS of them) from a "curious observer" space, to get a sense of what's really going on (without pre-judging the situation)

3. **It is NEVER too late to choose and change**. If something's not working for your teen(s)—or you as a parent—keep seeking something that will

# About the Author

Julie Oreson Perkins,
with her teens Connor and Christy

Julie Oreson Perkins, a certified life coach based in Boulder, CO, has often been affectionately described as "different." Through her dynamic conversations of change, energetic body work, and facilitation of "soulful time in nature," Julie invites service-based entrepreneurs and teen/parent teams to step up and into who they truly are... so they can create the changes they desire and live their lives *their* way. Using her keen insights and fostering the intuitive capacities of her clients, Julie serves as a guide to a more conscious, empowered life through individual and group coaching, webinars, nature retreats, speaking engagements, radio shows and her writings. She especially enjoys facilitating alongside her teens. Together they invite both parents and teens to explore the limitless possibilities for traversing the sometimes seemingly impassable terrain of teen-dom. Visit her at www.JulieOPerkins.com.

# Chapter 15

## Contribution the Kids Can Be

By Gosia Lorenz

In no way do I consider myself a parenting expert. According to the standards and judgments of this reality, many people wouldn't even consider me a good parent. And somehow, my boys have grown to become powerful, potent, curious, self-motivated, and... happy! This invites the question: What have we all decided it means to be a "good parent?" And, what if our children can actually turn out ok even if we don't fit that description?

Oh, the joy of becoming the parent! From the first moment of finding out the great news (YES! It was a happy day for my husband, Greg, and me—twice), through the delivery (won't bore you with the details), to today when I am a proud mama of two amazing boys, Ryvan (10) and Tracer (8).

I started off quite unprepared, I must admit. Growing up in communist Poland, surrounded by unhappy, suppressed

160

and repressed people, "conscious parenting" was an unknown phenomenon. My parents were loving and caring to me and did their best, no doubt about it. Conscious and aware? Not so much. They were much too busy arguing, bickering, blaming each other and hanging onto the past.

My mom, a typical Polish housewife who also had a full time job as a book keeper, did her best to have a normal life. My dad, an officer in the Polish army with a surprisingly keen interest in metaphysics and everything out of the ordinary, did everything to stay out of "this reality." Talk about growing up in a conflictual universe!

They took very good care of me, making sure that I was fed, warm and safe. Yet, when I look back at my childhood, they didn't teach me much about life and the world. I can't even recall hearing, "This is right, that is wrong. You should do this but not that." For years I was making them wrong for not giving me a moral compass, only to discover recently what a gift that was! I wasn't taught the basic foundations of judgment. The only advice I remember was: "Do you know how to count? Count on yourself" (my dad's pearls of wisdom), which pretty much shaped me up. I became independent and self-sufficient. As soon as it was legally permissible, (18 years old in Poland) I left my country and started traveling the world. Up to now I've lived in seven countries and had many adventures. Although this may not sound like a parenting book, it is fundamental to the way I set off on my parenting journey.

As I mentioned earlier, my dad was deeply involved in metaphysics and those were the obvious ideas about the world for him—UFOs, OOBE, holistic healing methods, life-after-life and conspiracy theories. I couldn't help but be interested in these things as well and implement these beliefs into my world of parenting. Mainstream and socially acceptable? No, not at all. I did everything to avoid the ordinary ways and to be different, to seek and question all the things that are unaccepted by an average, living, breathing person, and to go against everything that was a status-quo.

So here I am—a MOM. What? Me?! A mom?! The independent, rebellious, different, weird, yet blending-in-perfectly-when-required woman? Of course, I could not fall into a mainstream, traditional way of having children. I had to do it differently.

Attachment parenting—check

Co-sleeping—check

Nursing until my older son was three and a half and younger two years old—check

Total opposition toward substances I believed to be toxic, like vaccines—check

All organic foods—check

Homeopathic medicine when little bodies didn't feel well— check

All kinds of healer friends helping me with boys's well-being—check

I was so grateful for my husband, who, even though did not share my beliefs and ways, allowed me to choose what I was choosing at the time, and trusted that I knew what I was doing. I did not. I had bought so many controversial points of view, trusted every expert, teacher and authority on each subject, but never myself...

And then I discovered Access Consciousness®, when Ryvan was five and Tracer was three. It hit me like a lightning bolt. After studying all kinds of modalities and techniques my whole life (yes, I was seeking constantly) it felt like I had finally found home. The founder, Gary Douglas, and co-creator of Access, Dr. Dain Heer, inspired me in their way of facilitating people into their greatness and empowering them to know what they know. The tools of Access were easy, dynamic and profound. The changes that I was always asking for started occurring; the veils of the past started opening; the baggage began lifting off old programming and limitations were clearing. I began to perceive how much judgment I had been functioning from; how much right and wrong I had to have in place in order to judge that I was a perfect a mom; how inflexible and unaware I was with my boys. I lived in so much fear, anxiety, anger and stress. Even though I aligned and agreed with all things natural, I resisted and reacted to everything that was not. Good old polarity! Like the world can't function without it! No space for freedom, possibility, choice and happiness.

As I started using the tools of Access, I relaxed and eased into more allowance of everything that was not what I decided was right and correct. My friend once said, "If you don't have fun with your children, why have them?" It stopped me dead in the tracks: You mean children are not only responsibility, duty and sometimes even burden?! You can have FUN with them? You can play? Enjoy them? Have a good time? I totally missed that memo before! I chose to stop being such a control freak and have more fun with them and in life in general.

I began to see the gift my boys were and how fruitless it is to try to control them. My parents couldn't control me either, so there must be a way of functioning as a parent with more ease.

They are so brilliant and aware, and when I opened up to it, I could embrace the uniqueness, sweetness and contribution they were bringing to me and my life. I learned that I could simply ask them a question rather than tell them my point of view about something. They always surprised me with their awareness and what they seemed to know. Even though what they said was not always aligned with my point of view, it was light when they said it.

I realized how attuned the boys were to me. Each time I got stressed, irritated or overwhelmed by life, within minutes they were, too. I'm not always the brightest bulb in the box, so it took me a few years to realize that. They invited me to work on myself even more; to clear my limitations and heal old wounds. That old adage "Do as I say, not as I do" suddenly became so relevant to me.

I taught them the basic tools of Access right away. Tracer would find a penny on the ground, pick it up, say, "How does it get any better than this?" and put it in his pocket. When I would ask him who he was, he'd say, "I know! I'm an infeebeenie!"—toddler-speak for "infinite being."

I discovered that Ryvan, my older son, has capacities with entities and is very aware of them. Unfortunately he sometimes picks them up, too. I can look him in the eyes and see that he is not the only one in his body. His behavior changes dramatically and nothing that normally would work, works. He learned to recognize it as well and will now ask me to get rid of them. A few minutes of facilitation, and my boy is back.

I remember once we had a playdate with a friend I hadn't seen for a long time and her daughter in a beautiful, old park in Safety Harbor, Florida where we lived then. His behavior was getting worse by the minute. He was angry, mean, was running away from us, hiding and wouldn't listen. I was quite embarrassed and frustrated because he was taking all the attention and the playdate was not even remotely fun. In an attempt to change the tone of the day, we went on a little walk and climbed up a hill (a rare thing in a table-flat Florida). While on our trek, I read a little sign at the foot of the hill that disclosed, to my surprise, that we were playing in an old Native American sacred mound with, clearly, lots of dead Indians' spirits still hanging around. I knew immediately what was going on. We went to the car and Ryvan shouted, "Take them out of me!" So I used the entities clearing I learned in Access Consciousness and within a minute or two he was his smiling and sweet self. Who cares about how weird the tools are if they work, right?!

I love using the "light and heavy" tool. What feels light is true, what feels heavy is a lie. The boys know that they can't lie to mommy without me knowing, so sometimes when they both claim that they didn't do something, and clearly one of them did it, I'll simply ask the first one:

"Truth, did you do it?" — "No!" To the other one: "Truth, did you do it?" — "No!" Without a doubt, I can perceive the difference of the energy of both "NO's." One is light (he is telling the truth), one is heavy (he did it!). We usually end up laughing, the energy dissipates and the boys know that it's pointless to lie to mommy.

Even though they haven't learned all the Access Bars® points, I pay them $0.50 per minute to run my "implant band" and "restructuring of bodies." Ten to fifteen minutes with one of my potent boys is like an hour session with a grown up. They know that money can be easy and I trust that they will create wealth for themselves in the future. It is so beautiful how powerful these little people are. Huge beings with little bodies, full of wonder, possibility, joy, resilience and the willingness to move forward no matter what.

I love when they know when I'm trying to manipulate them and call me out on it. Even funnier is when they use the tools to manipulate *me*, like chanting together in the back of the car, "What would it take for mommy to buy us a toy? What would it take for mommy to buy us a toy?" until I start laughing and go buy them the toy (or whatever that is they ask for). I have told them many times that the tools work and it's a great manipulation on their part.

There are days when they are little crazy and I've had enough and the stress level rises. In the past, I would not be a fun person to be around. Now I ask questions: "What contribution can the boys be to me today? What contribution can I be to the boys today? What would it take for this to be easy and fun? Who am I being by being this way with them?" Something always shifts and things get easier.

One of my favorite tools of Access Consciousness is perceiving the future and making choices based on the awareness of what will they create 5-10-100 or more years from now for me and for the planet. Truth: If I choose this, what will my life be like five years from now? I perceive the energy of the future. Does it expand? Contract? Lighten up or get heavy? Next question: Truth: If I don't choose this what will my life be like five years from now? And again, I perceive the energy. I choose what's more expansive, light and joyful. I am sometimes surprised when I check the future of the boys and the choice I make based on this reality creates heaviness, and the choice that doesn't seem to make sense, creates lightness.

One of the situations I used this tool for was my trip to Costa Rica for an Access Consciousness 7-Day event. I kept asking, "What's the possibility to be there?" even though it didn't seem like I would make it that time. One day, very close to the event date, I asked if I could translate the class for Polish people that would be attending. I was beyond thrilled that the Universe delivered it once again! Then I started asking questions about the boys coming with me. The difference in the energy of the future for them and me was undeniably different, with huge expansion, lightness and joy for the boys coming. Once I chose this option, things lined up so they were included in my Costa Rica adventures. A whole week spent with beautiful people from all over the world seeking consciousness, and a group of children from Australia, changed them tremendously. To this day they tell me how free and happy they were there and ask me if they can go back someday. I can perceive a huge difference in their beings and way they show up in the world. They are so much more aware, potent and expanded.

I know that children, mine and other people's, are creating their own life and are way more aware than we give them credit for. People tend to look at them in a disempowering way and tell them how things *are* rather than ask them questions about what *they* know. Ryvan and Tracer attend a Waldorf school, and even though these schools are nurturing and holistic in their approach to children, Ryvan once said to me: "The school makes me forget everything I know." It was funny at the time, yet I know he is on to something and is aware of this reality.

One time when I was hosting my first class for Access Consciousness in Tampa, Florida, they both got very sick the night before. Suddenly they both had fevers and no energy, so there was no way I could send them to school. They joined us at the Level 2 and 3 Class. They slept and rested at the beginning and with each hour had more and more energy. Later on, they were ready to play with other children. In the evening they seemed almost back to normal so that I was planning to send them to school the next morning. To my surprise they both had the same symptoms that night and joined me at the class on the next day again. This time they had way more energy and fun and all the symptoms disappeared quickly. Do you think they created it to be with me at Access class? Yes! I have no doubt about it!

One of the tools of Access that comes in handy practically every day is muscle testing or "sway testing." When you stand up straight and ask your body to show you a "Yes" the body will sway forward. If you ask for "No," it will sway backwards.

I taught the boys this technique very early on and encouraged them to trust that their little bodies know what they need or require. They got really fast and good at it. If they ask for more cookies or other sweets I tell them to ask their body. When they do, sometimes it wants it and sometimes not. And there are times when they try to "cheat the system" and pull their body into yes when it's saying no. I can see it and we laugh and have a good time together. I use it to pick out supplements and natural remedies and to determine what amounts they require when their bodies are not feeling well.

We don't always have only ease, joy and glory during the day. Sometimes things get stressful and nobody is being conscious and aware. Questions save the day, even in those times. When they become a little crazy, I'll ask them, "Who are you being?" This invites them to be aware that they're not being themselves so they can snap out of it.

I noticed that when there is tension in the air or we are not happy, they will act it out with fighting, bickering or wrestling. They are amazing barometers of happiness or stress levels in the house and I'm so grateful that they are showing us that. I thank them daily for choosing me as their mom and they seem so proud for being acknowledged. When they were little, they would tell me stories of how they were looking at different people before coming to the Earth and saw mommy and daddy and knew that we would be the best parents for them.

An interesting thing showed up when I was writing this chapter. I was away from my boys for the longest time so far—11 days. I had chosen one of the most life-changing trips of my life—three Access Consciousness three-day classes in a row, held in Copenhagen, Denmark. I left the boys with my parents in Poland where we were spending six weeks of summer. Coming back light, expanded, happy and exploding with sense of possibilities and magic, it hit me like a 2X4 when my parents gave me a "little feedback." Apparently the boys (especially Ryvan) had not been "listening." They were doing what *they* wanted to do, and didn't want to read or do anything brainy and significant. All I heard was, "They don't do this and that, and *should* do this and that..." At that point, I almost gave up the writing of this chapter. I bought into the judgment and resisted what they were saying. I forgot about the tools, magic, possibilities, questions and choice. I was upset, bitter, disappointed and felt like the worst mom in the world in the face of my parent's judgment. My babies were being criticized! And it was all my fault because I didn't raise them right and didn't teach them to listen (notice the absence of question in that?) "I am wrong," and "I suck," and "Why on Earth did I choose to have them in the first place?" It was interesting how real their judgment seemed.

Then I did something terrible. I talked to Ryvan like a nagging, negative, and a NORMAL mom, making him wrong. On one hand, I knew that he was creating it, and it worked for him in some strange way (since he was the one creating it). On the other, I was not acknowledging how different he is and the fact that he was probably doing his best to make it for 11 days with my not-very-kind-to-each-other parents. He had entities and was sad and dark. I asked him some questions and cleared the entities while being aware that he pulled them from my mom's body to make her happier, or for whatever strange reason. All I could do to get my clarity back was to chant in my head, "All of life comes to me with ease and joy and glory," —the life-saving mantra of Access Consciousness, created by the brilliant Gary Douglas.

I got, once again, what a gift my son was. Once I became aware of what was really going on, I was able to see that neither of us were wrong, just aware. It made me wonder how many of us have been doing everything to make everyone around us happy to no avail, and have been made wrong for it?

I know I am not a perfect parent nor am I trying to be. I would have to judge myself constantly and compare myself to others or some utopian ideals that could never be true for me. I know there are many places where I could do a better job; I could cook more, play with them more (rather than work), read them more books or play more games... There is always more to be had and greater to create.

One thing I will do and be: I will continue to create a beautiful communion with my boys, and see them as a contribution and a brilliant gift, even in the challenging times, and know that they will change the world in one way or another. I have pledged to myself that I will not judge their choices in life and have their back no matter what. I will do anything to show them that being themselves is way more fun that trying to be someone else.

I am so grateful that these amazing beings chose my husband and me to share their lives with and it's such an honor to join them on their path. What would it take for me to be more like them in everyday life?...resilient, happy, curious, never giving up or giving in, and shooting for the stars!

# About the Author

GOSIA LORENZ

Gosia Lorenz was born and raised in Poland. Her interest in holistic health began at an early age when her father taught her how to use the divining rods and pendulums. She always knew there was more to life than she was told; that we are much more powerful and capable than we believe, and that different skills, which enrich life and improve health, can be learned. She continued her search throughout high school and while in college through attending multiple courses, classes (Silva Method™, Extrasensory Perception, Reiki, Dowsing and many others) and reading countless books on the above subjects.

By living in seven countries on three continents and traveling extensively, Gosia encountered many inspirational people and experienced a multitude of empowering moments. After she earned a Master's Degree in Tourism, she chose to pursue a career in holistic health and enriching people's lives. She studied BodyTalk Whole Healthcare™, Theta Healing™, Spiritual Health Coaching and was always searching for more.

In 2003, she moved to the United States and soon after,

was married. She is a mother of two boys, ten and eight years old.

After encountering Access Consciousness® in 2010, she immediately started using its tools and processes, which all proved to be highly effective. This was a missing link to all she had tried before. She became Access Consciousness Bars® Facilitator and very soon started facilitating Bars classes and trained hundreds of people in the United States and Poland over the last few years.

As an Access Consciousness Certified Facilitator she can facilitate classes on every subject under the sun, including: body, abundance, relationships, receiving, money, and more as well as The Foundation (formerly known and Foundation and Level 1) and Talk To The Entities® Classes that change lives all over the globe.

Gosia continues to develop her skills, broaden horizons, attend classes, and travel the world. She is always creating more. She knows that we can have it all; vibrant health and body, phenomenal life, endless possibilities and lots of ease and joy. She loves working with people from all walks of life who are looking for change. There is no issue, item, problem, program, implant, matrix, limitation, pattern, thought, feeling and emotion that she is unwilling to explore with her clients and clear if required.

Her life continues to expand and she is being a greater and greater contribution to the world around! What else is possible?!

# Chapter 16

## How Easy Can Parenting Be?

By Tanya Graham

I've been a parent for nearly 15 years to one child. I can tell you that using the tools of Access Consciousness® has brought more ease to my being, including being a mom. I didn't always have the tools, though. My husband and I started using them when my son was 11 years old. The ease we had before that came from following our knowing. The unease we had came when we doubted our knowing and bought what others told us.

There are so many points of view in the world about parenting: how long to nurse, at what age kids should be talking and walking, etc. What if, as a parent, you asked yourself, "What's going to work for my family? What do I know?" I bet you know plenty. What if my story doesn't tell you how to parent, but invites you to a different reality with your family? How cool would that be?

My son was born in a hospital, although I really wanted a homebirth. At the time, midwives were not readily available in my area and we couldn't afford one. My experience at the hospital was completely disempowering as I bought the point of view that I had to be a good little patient and not speak up. When the nurses whisked my bright-eyed baby away without asking, my gut said, "Do not allow this!" but I didn't stop them. My husband and I didn't think we had a choice or a voice, so we trusted and followed the hospital procedure. They put ointment in our baby's eyes and his eyelids became swollen and red, as if they had been burned. We felt terrible for welcoming our sweet little being into the world this way. He did not require that medicine. I did not have the diseases in my vagina that could lead to his blindness without the antibiotics. I was very angry about this standard procedure that didn't make any sense to administer to babies who weren't at risk. Instead of saying anything, I blamed myself for allowing it to occur. His pained gaze through the ooze is burned into my memory, as he demanded that I question conventional medicine when it came to his body. It took me years to let go of my anger about what had occurred and get to a place of gratitude about the situation. I get now how lucky I was that it was only a minor eye irritation with no long-term effects and that it invited me to always ask him and his body what he requires instead of allowing "authorities" to decide for us.

When it came to nursing, my son's tiny mouth struggled to accommodate my nipples and it was very uncomfortable for me. One mainstream book said the pain wouldn't last more than three months. This was not the case for me, and I thought, "What is wrong with me?" If I had listened to others I might have stopped breastfeeding and chosen formula. I chose, however, to embrace the intensity and allow my baby to choose when to wean. It was really important to me. The health benefits and vital bonding time outweighed my discomfort and by about five months it no longer hurt. At the time, the World Health Organization (W.H.O.) reported that 4.3 years was the average age that children stopped breastfeeding. Wouldn't you know it? My son stopped nursing at almost exactly that age. I wonder how much my point of view about that "average" age created my reality?

There is so much judgment about nursing and to what age. To this day, I can still silence a room of "open-minded" people who are pro-breastfeeding when I share that my son nursed until he was over four years old and that it is the world average. I actually don't talk about it much unless I am asked. There is judgment for those who choose not to breastfeed, those who do, and those who do if for X amount of months either being too little or too many. All these differing points of view suggest we are wrong no matter what we choose. I get that extended nursing is not for everyone. It's my point of view that some kids choose moms who choose not to breastfeed, some choose those who do for a little while, and some who do for a long time. What if you chose based on what works for you?

Self-weaning totally worked for *us*. I went back to work when my son was two months old, yet I nursed him full time. There were gasps of judgment from moms in the baby group who couldn't imagine leaving their babies at that age. They may have assumed I was away from him all day and that our relationship would suffer, but I had an amazing workplace that allowed us to choose to continue nursing even with my full time work schedule. I also had a husband who was a phenomenal stay-at-home dad who would bring our son in to nurse twice a day on a comfortable couch, surrounded by beautiful artwork. I was encouraged to take further breaks to pump and was welcome to store the breast milk in the staff fridge. Pumping was really easy for me. I didn't have to use a machine, just hold a container to catch the spray as I gently massaged. I was teased at work for having so much milk for such tiny boobs. It was ease for me to go back to work and continue to nourish and nurture my son.

When my son was a couple of weeks old, a nurse came to my home to observe us, weigh him, etc. She instructed me to talk to him more as I went about my day and told me that if I didn't he would have troubles with speech development. I thanked her for the information and told her I would do that. However, when I tuned into my son, I was able to acknowledge that he and I communicated through our minds, telepathically. If I had told that nurse what I knew, it would not have created something greater for my family. I may have been sent for psychiatric assessment. Sometimes, silence is golden! But if I had made her point of view mean more than what *I* knew, I might not have been willing to continue to communicate with my son in such an intimate way, nor would these skills have continued to develop for us.

What did I know about my son's capacity with communication? His ability to speak certainly did not suffer. His first word had two syllables, not one. He said, "kitty" one day after he crawled over to a soapstone sculpture of an obese cat at my workplace and patted its belly. Since then he has been extremely articulate with an extensive vocabulary, and a lover of the feline persuasion! Imagine if I had bought the nurse's point of view.

When it came to vaccinating our son, we chose not to. There is no right or wrong here. I made this decision based on my knowing. I didn't have the heavy and light tools that Access teaches, but I remember how heavy it was when I considered getting him the shots and that was how I knew it wasn't right for him. My doctor didn't ask me any questions about my decision, but instead told me all the horrible things that could happen and then called me naïve. I had actually spent hours researching both sides of the vaccine debate extensively so I would have the ammunition to defend my choice, but I chose not to fight. Instead, I chose a different doctor. This was another instance where I was grateful for our eye ointment incident in the hospital. If I hadn't chosen then to choose what we truly believe is best for us, we may have been guilted into choosing something that didn't feel right for us. I was empowered to realize that we always have choice.

My son, like most children, is very aware. He has a capacity with entities. He perceives energies and he can read minds. He is also very private about it and mostly only shares this with my husband and me. He used to talk about a previous life and his "momma on the mountain." One time, when he was four, he perceived my bizarre craving. I was eating my nut-butter sandwich thinking, "Mayonnaise would taste good on this," although at the time I didn't use mayo. He abruptly got up from the kitchen table, scrambled to the very back of the fridge, grabbed a jar of mayo jar that belonged to our roommate and passed it to me saying, "Here momma!" I looked him square in the eye and said in my head, "If you can hear me, tell me you love me." He responded with a grin and said, "I love you momma!" I was excited and I hugged him and thanked him for choosing me. I know how much of a contribution it is to have our capacities celebrated. Imagine having someone in your life that doesn't judge you, no matter what comes up, no matter how strange it is. Imagine being that someone for your kids. This also confirmed to me that my awareness of the vaccines and eye ointment not working for him was real and not something I made up. It gave me even more confidence to continue to honor my knowing and choose what worked for us.

When my son was born, my husband and I practiced a strict diet. Our family didn't eat meat for seven years. That was one area where I wasn't listening to my body but rather what others had decided was a healthy choice. Ha! There was no "choice" in my diet as it eliminated so many foods. I was very controlling and our son didn't get sugar until he was over two because I was attempting to do it right! Nowadays, after learning Access tools, we eat what our bodies require, including sugar, salt and water. We don't buy the points of view anymore that our son's recurring desire for macaroni and cheese isn't healthy, that candy will rot his teeth, or that French fries are bad for him. Our son asks his body what to eat when he's hungry and there are no battles about food. Imagine giving up all of your points of view about food and having total choice with it. What would this create for you and your kids?

What else do I know about parenting my only child? A family bed totally worked for us. We were told that it was dangerous for baby and not good for us as a couple. I didn't buy it and would respond with, "It's not for every family." It created ease for us to eliminate the separate crib, especially in the early months when my son nursed every few hours. Later, when I returned to work, I was able to sleep and nurse and snuggle my son at night, all in the comfort of our family bed. We continued the closeness that others judged me for giving up by returning to work. But I didn't have to get up! It was brilliant. One time we attempted putting him in the crib, but it led to an eerie incident with a broken musical toy that suddenly started playing through the baby monitor, and us quickly bringing him back into our room. It didn't work for him to be away from us. By the time he was eight years old, he was ready for his own bedroom, and he never looked back.

When it came to Santa Claus, the Easter Bunny and the Tooth Fairy we knew our son perceived the stories as lies, so we chose to be honest. It created more for him to be told the truth so he could trust *his* knowing. If we had lied, we would have been asking him to give up his knowing and that wasn't something we saw value in choosing. I was judged for taking away the magic of Christmas by another mom. I shared with her that he and I talked about the magic of everyday miracles, of gratitude, and of our abilities to heal bodies, but she wasn't willing to hear that. She was concerned he would ruin it for her kids. We asked him to keep it to himself and he never told another child. My son still reaped the benefits of gifts under the tree, chocolate treasure hunts and rewards for losing teeth, but we told him it came from us. He was very grateful and we received the thanks. How does it get any better than this?

I used to have some very interesting points of view about technology. I bought the idea that electronic devices were damaging to developing brains, so we didn't watch television when my son was little. When we finally got a computer, our son was introduced to video games for the first time and his capacity for technology was undeniable. I remember choosing to let go of my beliefs after I recognized I was being like the dad who wouldn't acknowledge his son's ability to dance because he wanted him to be a jock. I realized that forcing my son to stay away from technology didn't make any sense. Since using the tools of Access, our son decides how much computer time he gets. For fun, he has developed an app, a video game, and spent hundreds of hours learning how to code. He is fourteen now and well on his way to his target of being a computer programmer.

Not only does he choose his computer time, our son also chooses his bedtime. It wasn't always like this, however. We used to put him to bed on school nights at a certain time although it was much later than the bedtime of most kids. It was always a struggle to get him to fall asleep. Even as a little guy, he was a night owl. He could also function on very little sleep and it didn't affect his behavior the next day. We noticed some parents dealt with monsters if their child didn't get enough sleep. This "go to bed when you want to" thing really works for us! I encourage him to ask his body what it requires since it changes all the time. He's used to asking questions to bring himself awareness. He has also taught himself how to fall asleep fast and control his dreams. How much fun does he have at night?

My son also gets to choose his homework situation. This school year is nearly over and the total time he has done schoolwork at home is less than an hour, yet he's on the Principal's List. He is a smart kid, but the ease comes from his awareness. I used to be a smart kid too, but my A's were obtained from hours upon hours of homework. I bought that good marks came from studying. Thankfully, I have given up this point of view that he didn't buy anyway. He also gets his Bars® run, especially after he picks up the anxiety from other kids before exams or papers are due. Sundays used to be hell when he was aware of everyone's shit about Mondays; their not wanting to go back to school, or work, or whatever. The Bars has changed that and created so much ease for him. Now he looks forward to school, is able to identify when he requires to have his Bars run and will ask for a session.

What else do I know? Consciousness includes everything and judges nothing, including boys with long hair! My son has total hippy hair, straight out of the seventies, with big, luscious curls that hang down his back. If we had listened to a few of his grandparents, we would have forced him to cut it. He's been called a girl more than once. This has never bothered him. In fact, he recounts the story about being referred to as a friend's sister, with laughter. He sees the humor of the people who mislabel him out of total unawareness. He is so comfortable being him that the judgments he gets float right through him. How cool is that?

Our son, like everyone, is different, yet he was always comfortable being different. He used to go to kindergarten class with his shirts purposely on backwards. He had fun with that signature look for a while. At five, his favorite color was pink. We chose to embrace it and get him pink shirts, a pink bike, etc. I am so grateful that my husband went along with this, as I remember some male friends suggesting that we were creating a sissy. Did we create a sissy? Or something else?

I'm reminded of the time our son was in kindergarten and chose to dress up as a unicorn for Halloween. His costume was soft and fluffy and quite feminine according to this reality. The other boys, who were dressed as superheroes and firemen, approached him. One of them said, with nasty sarcasm, "Nice pink fur!" Without hesitation, my son replied, "It's not pink, it's mauve!" with a tone suggesting that this boy was an idiot for not identifying the correct color and the attitude of, "You want a piece of this luxurious, cuddly unicorn? Oh, yeah you do!" At that point, the bullying ceased and every boy reached out to gently pet the wispy mane of my son's unicorn costume. My son melted their worlds that morning, by being him.

I have always spoken to my son like he's an adult, rather than a child. I didn't do baby talk and I certainly don't sugarcoat my language, but that's just me. I wonder which gets more judgment: profanity or baby-talk? I swear when it's required, to deliver intensity, and sometimes when it's not required. Interestingly, he never cusses. I have thrown a hundred dollar bill on his bed and begged him to say, "shit," just for the sake of it, but he won't. I find it hilarious and I love sharing this! How many judgments does this bring up about me being a bad parent or about him being a good kid? It's just a game and what would it take to be able to offer him a million dollars to cuss? How much fun would that be?

It might sound like our son is spoiled. Yep, he is. He gets to make choices about his clothes, his bedtime, his computer time, and his food. The thing is, his choices work for us and the coolest thing is he got to choose us! How lucky are we? Despite the fact that I can't get him to swear, even if I ask him to read "push it" fast (he saw right through that), I am still willing to be the master manipulator of the family. Yes, he came here to torture me and control me, but I call him on that. When he's a little shit I call him on it. I am willing to be the worst parent in the world. When he's an angel, I call him on it and I'm willing to be the best parent in the world. Would you be willing to be everything and nothing for your kids? I wonder if that would create more ease for you and your family?

I thank my son for choosing me all the time! It creates ease in our lives. Sometimes I have fun with it if he gets frustrated with me. I can choose to respond with frustration or I can choose to sincerely say, "Thank you for choosing me!" My gratitude for him can melt his world. I wonder what gratitude can do for you?

Being a parent keeps getting easier and easier the more points of view I don't buy. I seriously get giddy about how easy it can be when we give up parenting based on others' expectations. What if we acknowledged that parenting doesn't have to be hard? What if we acknowledged the areas of parenting we have ease with, to invite more ease? What if we asked with curiosity and wonder, "How easy can parenting be?" What would that create? Hmmmmm... I wonder.

# About the Author

TANYA GRAHAM

Tanya Graham is an Access Consciousness® Bars Facilitator currently living in Summerland, British Columbia, Canada. She enjoys playing and creating with people, paint, art, words, voice and music. As well as offering private Bars® sessions and classes to those who desire to receive, she is an artist, photographer, author and singer/songwriter. You can find out more about Tanya's practice, her artwork and music at www.TanyaGrahamArt.com.

# Chapter 17

## Welcome to Where?!

BY DANIELLE VARANDA

When I look back in my life, as well as look forward into the future with my 19-year-old special-needs daughter Sofia, what comes to mind is an article that my mother gave me right after she turned 11 months old and it had become apparent that she was not reaching the "age-appropriate milestones." Soon after, it was determined that she had "global developmental delays." However after age six, they labeled her with "Mental Retardation."

One of the many letters sent into *Dear Abby*, "Welcome to Holland" was written by a woman named Emily Perl Kingly. When she was asked how it was raising a special needs child, she wrote this article in response. To summarize, she compares planning and expecting the joyous event of having a baby to planning and expecting a much anticipated dream vacation. She likened it to planning a trip to Italy, where all of your friends have either gone or are going. You're so excited to explore this country and all the wonderful things there that you have heard about. After years and months of anticipating the trip, you arrive to this amazing place, and as the plane lands, you hear the flight attendant announce, "Welcome to Holland."

"What? Holland?"

This is was not the trip that I had planned! I didn't sign up to go to Holland! I wanted to go to Italy like everyone else! The two are so different, you could never really relate to all of your friends that went to see Italy or talk about their shared experiences.

So began my imperfect adventure with my daughter, and my imperfect life that I had tried so hard to make so perfect.

Or was this really what I had been asking the Universe for all along? Something, and someone, to show me a different possibility? I mean after all, I always knew I was different, and somewhere I was asking for a different possibility and a different reality. And can I just say, having a child with special needs does create a different reality beyond *this* reality!

Even though this was years before I had Access Consciousness® come into my life, I had been asking for change. I had trouble conceiving after having my first child, and had made a pact with God that if he granted me a child I would do anything, like stop drinking. Of course, when I became pregnant with her, I did not hold up my end of my bargain and did not stop drinking, even during her pregnancy... the terrible secret, which no one could know except my husband at the time.

Sofia was in distress during labor, and then ended up having the cord wrapped around her neck twice when she was born. Although there is nothing on her birth chart to indicate that she had oxygen deprivation, I now know that this was one of two things that created her the way she was, as well as the way she developed during the pregnancy.

Even though at her birth no one else raised any suspicion of there being anything different about her, I knew... there was something different about her. Yes she was a Double D: definitely different. Her Apgar score was very low after delivery and I recall hearing the doctor say, "Breathe baby breathe." Soon after, her Apgar score went to the more normal range. And yet, when they were checking her vitals and washing her she was very quiet, where most babies will scream and protest. Instead, we went into the conclusion that this just meant she was a good baby. What did I know that I was not willing to know?

At her three-month check up with her pediatrician, I brought to his attention how her eyelids were a bit quirky in their movement, which we thought was very cute, by the way, especially when she nursed or took a bottle and they would pulse wider as she sucked. So cute! It wasn't until my mention of it that he acknowledged that there could be something different about her. I remember this as the moment when I stepped into my advocacy of my daughter. I realized that I knew more about my daughter than her pediatrician, and I still know more than he does about her. This is something I share to this day. Always go with your own knowing, no matter what! Even if it is a child expert. Even if it is a doctor. Know that you know!

So began my unexpected trip to Holland; landing in a foreign country that I never had planned to visit.

Our first stop was at the therapy sessions and doctor's visits with specialist after specialist: Occupational therapist, Children's Ophthalmologist, Eye Muscle specialist, Birth to 3 Center twice a week. Here Sofia received one-on-one sessions with a speech therapist, physical therapist, a special education teacher and the Neurologist that headed up the birth to three center.

At first I did not know or understand the language of this place. Then over time, bit by bit, I became more familiar with the language. It was through the experience of being a mother of Sofia that I learned to ask a lot of questions.

But oh! The shame and the wrongness I felt with having a special-needs child! Not to mention the secret shame and guilt that I had thinking I had caused it from having drank during her pregnancy. I now know that none of that actually belonged to me. I was just aware of everyone else's projections, expectations and judgments. Everything I thought I "felt" at that time was just stuff I was picking up from others, and then buying as mine. And what was right about this that I was not getting?

So through this foreign, unknown territory, I began to find my way around and realized that I was the expert of Sofia more than any of the experts.

Now, more about this sweet, adventure known as my daughter, Sofia. Well, "adventure" is definitely a great description! And she was sweet as well... until she was two and a half-years-old.

She truly enjoyed everything and everyone around her. She would laugh and smile and was a true delight. For some curious reason, she loved to watch people eat and watch anything that was boiling on the stove. I never did quite get that, and yet it was part of what made her delightful: her quirkiness. There was something extra special about her being a baby for a lot longer than most parents usually get with their children.

Then all of that shifted one day. You know those days you are so tired and overwhelmed and just want to go to sleep and they won't? I was so frustrated with her that I got mad and I yelled at her to go sleep (of course that did not work very well... more shame and guilt).

The reason I bring this up is not just to point out what judgments I had of myself as an imperfect mother; it was that I realized that it was a turning point with Sofia, that she was different after that. She changed after that and was not the sweet, delightful little girl she used to be. Now you can say the two's going into three's can be difficult. However, this was more of a nightmare.

I do not recall all the annoying, challenging things that she started doing; I have blocked most of it out. However, the one I remember the most, probably because it was the worst, was that she learned how to spit. And she had amazing accuracy. Now I do not know if you have ever been spit on, but I know for a fact, it has been used throughout history as a sign of disrespect. Spitting is used in many countries as the ultimate insult. The energy of it, as well as the physical aspect, is quite disgusting; different energy than vomit, but up there in the disgust department. It's also different because one is deliberate and the other is involuntary from not feeling well. I guess you could equate it to being in a foreign country where they have very odd behaviors and things you find rude just because it does not fit with what your point of view might be.

And then, just to add another layer, when we would be out and about, she would spit on other people at any given moment! For me this was worse than any horror movie I had ever seen. And let's just talk about the JUDGMENT! (Notice how I put those in capital letters?) I was so aware of other people projecting their disdainful judgments onto Sofia, and to me as her mother. Of course, Sofia didn't care. She just turned it up on those that had the most judgments, which were the ones she tended to spit on.

So I bring all of this up for two main reasons. One is that it wasn't until about four years ago, when I discovered the tools of Access Consciousness that I realized that Sofia is what is called a "walk-in." When the "being" in the body, for various reasons, sometimes due to extreme stress (like when mommy is being a rage monster), decides it does not want to stay in the body and chooses to leave, another being without a body can come in. When this occurs, there often is a major shift in personalities.

So there were many years of finding my way through this foreign land, where you just have to know that you know more than you think you do. You are not nearly as "fucked up" as you think you are! No matter how much judgment you are perceiving from everybody else. Even when you are judging yourself for not knowing what to do with a special-needs child that does not care what anybody thinks and is a transformative agent of magnitude.

Which reminds me of the other behavior that Sofia would do, especially out in public: she would give people "the bird" and say, "Fuh ahh!" Which was another judgment-magnet of magnitude! I could always perceive she did this with the people who were in the most judgment of that word. Well! How aware is she?! How much does she facilitate for others? How much does she invite people into question, even if that question is, "WHAT? REALLY?" and, "WHAT THE...?" Her speciality is "Wedge and Walk."

Have you ever been in another country where you were unclear of where to go or how to communicate? You might have been very uncomfortable, and then someone kind and caring came up to you and helped you? S/he may not have even spoken the same language as you, but they spoke the language of the heart. I have so much gratitude for these people that showed up in Sofia's and my life. Sometime they were adults and sometimes they were children. Overall they shared one thing in common, what I used to refer to as an "open heart." I now refer to them as "having their barriers down and in total allowance of Sofia."

I had an astrological reading of Sofia's chart when she was not quite four years old. I will always remember them saying, "Well, it may be true that she is not of average intelligence. However personally, I believe intelligence is highly overrated in this country. She has the intelligence of the heart; actually, the genesis of the heart." Her chart also indicated, what I believe is called, "The finger of God," which is the ability to transform others on a level of magnitude!

I was aware of how beautiful that was, even though I did not completely comprehend it at that time. And boy can she change things! I see how she was the gift that invited me to step into other possibilities that I may not have not have done otherwise, such as alternative medicine, energy work and the modalities that eventually led me to find the tools of Access Consciousness... as well as sobriety, just to name a few.

When I first heard of the book, *Would You Teach A Fish To Climb A Tree?* by Anne Maxwell, Gary Douglas and Dr. Dain Heer, I thought, "What a stupid title for a book!" No judgment there! Until I got the book and found where the title came from. It is a quote from Albert Einstein. "Everybody is a genius. But if you judge a fish by its ability to climb a tree, it will live its whole life believing that it is stupid." Actually, what may be more accurate than that is, we will "believe that" they are stupid. I mean, isn't that how we translate the label of mental retardation? What if we are the ones that are slow and they know more than we do?

Speaking of labels... the other quote I love to share from that book is, "A Word About Labels," a quote from Gary Douglas: "Don't define these children by their labels. You will cut off your receiving of what they have to gift to you. Instead ask a question. 'What is the gift they have that I am not receiving?'"

I cry every time I share that with someone.

Speaking of receiving... how much have I received from Sofia that I am not even aware of? How much is she a gift that I have not been willing to receive? How much do all of us do this in so many areas of our lives?

How much have I received from Sofia that I *do* acknowledge? The beautiful, the good, the bad and the ugly? It may not always be comfortable or pretty, however it can be amazing just the same!

Being a parent of Sofia has certainly been challenging; and more often than not, difficult. It was especially hard on my marriage. Although she is not the reason her dad and I are no longer married, it did take a toll.

I also know it has been a different experience for her two brothers, than for their friends with siblings. My oldest son, who is seven years older than Sofia, knew life before she was born. My youngest son is seven years younger than her, and has only known life with Sofia. They have also had their challenges with her. However, there is something kinder and gentler about them as a result of having Sofia as a sister.

Another area I had to eventually become willing to change my point of view was about being her primary caregiver, and to finally allow other people to take care of her. What could she receive from other people that I was not able (or willing) to give? Of course, it required letting go of the judgment that I had around being a "good mother" and that I "should be" her primary care-provider. How many points of view was I picking up from other people around that? A little, a lot, or a mega ton? Probably a mega ton!

We have been so fortunate to have had many wonderful care-providers over the years for Sofia, and I am so grateful for them all! We sometimes struggled to find a good match; someone who was in allowance of Sofia and not in judgment of her or what judgment she might bring up for them.

During a time when I was struggling with being a mom to Sofia, and not being able to give her what she seemed to require, another Access facilitator suggested that I might want to ask Sofia (telepathically) where she would like to live. Of course, I asked her verbally, to which she responded, "I don't know." Then I asked her telepathically, and a month later, like magic, an amazing care-provider showed up! Soon after, she started staying with her part time. I am totally aware that Sofia created this. How amazing is she? How much has she always been the gift that I required her to be in my life? How much has she always created everything she required in her life?

When she first started staying with her care-provider and with her dad, I felt guilty because I did not see her very much. When I shared this with a friend in Access, she responded, "Do you really feel guilty?" I realized that, no, I did not! I was just very aware and was just picking up on everybody's points of view of what it means to be a "good mother."

Even though I found myself in a different foreign country that I was not expecting to ever visit, I was able to receive the beauty, the gifts and the transformation that it had to offer; the gift that no one other than Sofia had to offer to me, and everyone else she has encountered.

As I like to say, when Sofia is happy, everybody is happy!

# About the Author

DANIELLE VARANDA

Danielle Varnada has always been called to areas of transformation. For over 30 years she has been the owner of Essential Jade, specializing in skincare and nail care as a licensed esthetician. She is also the owner of International Feng Shui Design as a certified Blue Mountain Feng Shui consultant. As well, she is an Access Consciousness® Certified Facilitator and has known that something else was possible. In this adventure called her life, Danielle is known as the "Transformative-agent-of-magnitude," transforming her life as well as the lives of others.

She resides in Seattle, and in San Francisco, and has 3 amazing children who have transformed her life beyond her wildest imagination!

You can get in touch with Danielle here:
Daniellevaranda.accessconsciousness.com
Internationalfengshuidesign.com
Essentialjade.com

# Chapter 18

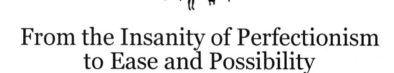

## From the Insanity of Perfectionism to Ease and Possibility

BY KATHY WILLIAMS

Growing up in the world of ballet, I was trained to strive for perfection. While this helped me to refine my art and achieve a level of mastery, it also became my undoing—creating a spiral of judgment and frustration about my body and it's inability to achieve the look that I strived tirelessly to attain. The insanity of perfectionism that ultimately led me to stop dancing is not unique to artists. It can rear its ugly head in any area of our lives. As my parenting journey illustrates, when we are able to overcome the need to "get it right," (according to whom?) we become free to allow our own innate wisdom to lead the way.

Even before my son was born, I had definite beliefs about how I'd parent; what I'd say, and do, and what I'd never do. Like many new parents, I wanted to get everything right for my son, to provide the best possible environment for him to grow into a strong, wise, capable person. I had no inkling that my conclusions about the right way to parent would cause suffering to both me and my children, and that ultimately we would re-emerge from that experience into a way of being that involves following our own knowing rather than any external philosophy or method.

For baby's arrival into the world, I had arranged to have a natural tub birth at a birthing center attached to a hospital. The center provided midwives and a cozy environment, complete with a Laura Ashley bedspread, lace curtains, and a giant bathtub. I prepared for the experience by doing prenatal yoga and listening to a guided visualization CD several times a day. Despite my wishes, preparations, and expectations, after 25 hours of painful back labor, I ended up having a C-Section in the hospital.

To temper baby's transition from the watery womb into a world of light and innumerable stimuli, I chose to room in for 40 days. This is a tradition suggested by Ayurveda, the holistic medicine system of India, which is considered the sister science to yoga. The idea is a sort of honeymoon, but with your baby—a "babymoon" during which you are nurtured and pampered while you recover your strength from childbirth and focus on your new little one. While this six-week period had promised to be a time of rejuvenation, nurturing and bonding with my baby, without the distraction of the external world, it also turned into a trip of a different kind: a guilt trip, where I marinated in feelings of regret and frustration about not providing the "perfect birth" for my baby. Where the heck were my doting aunties from India, to cook nourishing foods and massage me and baby with warm herbalized oils? Time at home did allow me to meditate, heal and connect inwardly. But as the weeks rolled on, I became stir-crazy, suffocating

from lack of interaction with the outside world. To minimize
the strain on baby's developing senses, my only outings were
to the OB and the pediatrician, and rarely, a quick dip into the
grocery store. With great relief, several days shy of the 40-day
allotment, baby and I came up for air and joined my husband
on a short trip to visit friends.

By the time my son was two years old, I realized that he
had arrived on the planet in the way that was right for him;
he likely wouldn't be irreparably damaged having been born
by C-Section as my birth-preparation class had indicated he
might. When he was two and a half, I put him in a Waldorf-
inspired six-child "playschool" two mornings a week, to give
me a few uninterrupted hours to read, and write, stretch, and
hike. The move to a town 40 minutes away didn't deter me; I
was a "good mother" after all, and willing to make sacrifices of
time and energy for him to go to a suitable school.

I had definite fixed points of view about what kind of
school was suitable, largely informed by attending "mommy
and me" classes and a weekend seminar on "care of the very
young child" at a popular Waldorf school. We were urged to
seek out a home-like setting, and to favor naturally made toys
that engaged the imagination, rather than plastic toys with
bells and whistles. Though I interviewed a dozen places in
my town, none of them met my strict standards. So, we drove
40 minutes each way up the hill two days a week so he could
attend a half day of school.

Somewhere along the line, I had read that more than a
half-day of school would be stressful on a young child, so of
course, I couldn't inflict that sort of unnecessary stress on
him. Instead I inflicted it on myself, with a long drive and little
time for self-rejuvenation.

While constantly considering my son's needs and choosing
what I deemed best for him, I didn't stop to consider what

would really work for me. This wasn't true in every way. I was willing to hire a babysitter to have a weekly date night with my husband—but most of the time, I put my preschooler's needs above my own. In my mind, I couldn't justify spending the money for more babysitting time if I wasn't earning anything myself. And I wouldn't spend enough time away from my child to do the work I loved—a delightful catch-22! Thankfully, by the time baby #2 was born, a friend had introduced me to a lovely preschool in our neighborhood, (that did, horror of horrors, have a few plastic toys) and I had adapted to the idea of him attending from 9 a.m. to 3 p.m.

When my second baby was on his way, I was determined not to have another C-section, both for baby's sake and my own. The nearby hospital wouldn't allow that, so I chose to go to the island of Oahu from my home on Maui to give birth. For weeks, I practiced self-hypnosis, and eventually flew to Honolulu with my son to wait for baby to arrive. We didn't have to wait long! My contractions began early the next morning, and I labored for four hours, watching the horizon turn from dark to light while my son slept in the bedroom. Baby was on his way sooner than expected. None of my family was yet on island, so we called some family friends. Fortuitously, Tuesday was the husband's day off; he was able to drive me to the hospital while his wife looked after my son. Once I was settled into my room at Moanalua Medical Center, baby popped out within 40 minutes. If my husband hadn't been the last one off the airplane, he might have been there to witness the event. This time, after birth, I did my best to keep baby protected from excessive noise, bright light and wind, but I did not remain a shut-in for 40 days.

Still convinced that my family must use Waldorf principles or my children might turn into video-game playing derelicts, I followed the recommendations I had learned. Speaking in low voices, playing games of song and rhyme, and no TV, I could implement easily. The emphasis on rhythm and routine, and the limit of only one or two outings per week so as not to overwhelm the child's developing faculties were more challenging...

And the suggestion to work with the hands? I had put together a child's wagon once. I think the wheel fell off the next day. Another time I made my way through knitting half a scarf before I grew tired of the project. Work with the hands, whether carpentry or crochet, was never really my forte. Typing? That I could do. Not quite the kind of handwork they were talking about; all things technological are viewed with disdain in Waldorf. It was not for lack of trying. At the aforementioned "mommy and me classes," we parents sewed and felted quietly, watching as the wee ones built towers, played dress-up, and pushed dolls in buggies. It was a sweet time, but I always felt like a bit of a misfit. Felting and crafting were enjoyable enough during the class, but I had little desire to do such things at home. My creativity has less to do with crafts than with creating workshops and classes, things that are fun for my playful, interactive nature.

Limiting my outings with my new baby and preschooler began to wear on my nerves. The boys didn't nap in unison, so I was generally active with one of them, even though I sorely lacked the sleep that mothers of new babies so desire. Finally, I welcomed my mother's suggestion that 30 minutes of PBS cartoons could be good for all of us! However short, I needed that mid-day rest from the energy and ingenuity required keep a bright, curious three-year-old boy busy from morning until night. When he wasn't actively engaged in an activity of interest, he took up the hobby of gently flapping his baby brother's ears. Apparently he was seeking more stimulation, too.

We abandoned the "limit outings to one or two times per week" guideline, to save my sanity. And guess what? We all became happier. Playgroups had new toys for the kids, and women with whom I could have a real conversation. We all had new stimuli to spark our interest. As I became less rigid and embraced more of my own relaxed parenting style that brought more ease for me, we all benefitted. What if choosing happiness is one of the most important things we can model for our children? Your happiness matters, and the energy of that happiness ripples out into interactions with family, and beyond.

After I started using the tools of Access Consciousness®, I learned the concept that every "should" or "should not" is simply an interesting point of view. This frees us from the idea that someone else's philosophy or method is better than our own way and our own awareness. This also allowed me to have peace around letting go of my "Waldorf Roots." I realized that the serenity of working on hand crafts that have no application to practical life may truly make some women happy. And that's great! For me, it was just another place to feel inept while still striving for perfection.

Imagine how different my life would have been, if, when trying to follow the principles from books or classes, I had asked, "Does this suggestion work for us?" or, "While this may be great for some people, how is it working for my family?" If I had been willing to ask, "What would work for me?" or "How would I like my life to be?" I could have reduced my self-inflicted suffering. Buying into what I thought was the "right way" because it was what I saw "conscious parents" doing was, in fact, not a very conscious choice.

Functioning from conclusion, rather than question, I believed that others must know better than I do about nurturing small beings into wise, well-adjusted people. Indeed, seeing kind, intelligent children emerge from the Waldorf philosophy is what inspired me to choose it for my own family. By sharing my story, I am not trying to criticize any method or philosophy. I'm simply inviting you to use question, awareness and self-trust to know what works for you. If I had questioned each element, "Does simplifying the child's environment work for me?" (Yes) "Does staying inside?" (No), I could have received the elements that were useful to me, and discard those that weren't, without making myself wrong for not entirely fitting into a set of guidelines that had been put together decades before my birth. On some level, I've always known that life flows more easily when I follow my own wisdom. Yet I had abandoned that wisdom because parenting seemed like such a big task, and I surely didn't want to mess up my kids!

A huge gift I have received from Access Consciousness is the ability to remain in a space of continuous question in my life, with my kids and beyond.

When the kids are in a funky mood, I might ask, "Is it fun to be like Eeyore (or irritable Rabbit)? Or would you like to be happy?" I've even asked, "Would you rather cry, or would you rather color? What do you choose?" It helps them realize that in every moment, they can choose how to be, what to do, and how to respond. When they're upset, I may also ask, "What are you aware of?" We're so hugely aware, (even people in tiny bodies) and more aware than we give ourselves credit for! When kids are out of sorts, it's very possible that they may be picking up on other people's thoughts, feelings, or emotions. Or when I ask about their awareness, they may recognize the discomfort of hunger, thirst, or the need to pee.

Each of us has been given this amazing gift called choice. Yet how many of us were taught that we're constantly choosing how to be, what to be, what to do, and where we're putting our attention? I so wish someone had taught me that early on! I often ask my kids, "If you choose that, what will it create?" before they select an activity, or after they've done something like call brother a name. This way they start to recognize that each action creates something, either toward or away from the future they desire, and they can learn to trust their own knowing.

This doesn't mean the kids are in charge of everything we do. But they are in charge of their responses to it. When the kids desire or do something I don't prefer, I like to respond, "That doesn't work for me." If they question or protest, I can explain more, or just repeat, "That just doesn't work for me." There no real need to explain further. Usually one "that doesn't work for me," is enough to stop an undesirable behavior in it's tracks.

Have you ever heard that parenting is the hardest job you'll ever have? I had bought that point of view, and because your point of view creates your reality. For several years, I suffered under the burden of "the hardest job ever." When I realized that point of view was making life harder than it needed to be, I wrote a simple reminder on the chalkboard in the kitchen: "How can I have ease and fun with parenting?"

Seeing this simple question in big yellow letters, several times a day changed a lot for me. While juggling cutting vegetables and keeping two kids from bickering, I could glance over and remind myself to ask, "How can I have ease and fun with parenting?" We shift our energy when we ask questions!

This question inspired me to be more creative even with the annoying questions that kids like to ask. When my husband was at work and my youngest would ask, "Where is daddy?" for the third time, I'd answer, "On the moon... In a tree... Underground... On a boat." Being playful provided freedom from the drudgery of repeating, "He's at work," again, and again, and again. Nonsense responses are a huge gift when a child constantly asks, "Why?" It becomes a game. What kind of ridiculous answer can I come up with next?

My hope is that reading about my foibles, ludicrous as they look in retrospect, will reinforce that fitting ourselves into a set system, (even a great system) may promise a sense of ease, yet create the opposite effect. Blindly following anything makes us exactly that, blind. It requires us to cut off our own awareness. What if your parenting journey—one that's never been lived before—is a creative endeavor that will stretch you, and expand you, and delight you more than trying to live anyone else's way ever could? After all, what other job requires us to be chauffeur, chef, reader, storyteller, counsellor, cop, cleaning person, nurse, educator, and more? (Have you acknowledged all the things you do)? What if listening to our innate wisdom and awareness will allow us to be and create magic with the magical beings who have entrusted us with their care?

# About the Author

KATHY WILLIAMS

Kathy Williams, CFMW, is an Access Consciousness® Certified Facilitator, Transformational Coach, and Yoga Therapist. Since 2000, Kathy has been sharing tools and techniques that empower people to move beyond physical and emotional pain and into lives of joyous possibility.

From new businesses and careers, to raises; from meeting a partner, to creating a life, Kathy is a master at helping people get what they want. Her clients are from all over the globe and range from the very young to individuals in their 80's. Well-versed in the ancient wisdom practices of breath, movement, and meditation, as well as the practical, effective energetic tools of Access Consciousness, Kathy brings with her not only her wealth of knowledge but also her ebullient joy and uncanny ability to zero in on the most potent tool to apply to get the greatest result. She works with clients by phone and in person on Maui, where she also creates personalized retreats for people to unwind and create a reset for their lives.

For years, Kathy worked toward her goal of dancing the

principal roles in ballets such as *Romeo and Juliet,* and *The Nutcracker.* Although she was able to procure the prestigious roles she had dreamed of, her desire for perfection (a goal that can never be attained) prevented the happiness and sense of success she always thought would accompany such roles. When she realized this, Kathy began to reassess her life and her direction. She recognized how vital it was to her to create happiness in everyday moments—not as some future to strive toward but never attain. Now she empowers clients with simple, effective tools that they can use to move beyond the need to get life perfect, so they can enjoy ease and joy everyday and create lives beyond their imaginings.

Kathy's target is to increase the joy on the planet. As each of us taps into our natural joy and happiness, we spread that wherever we go.

Read more of her story in the best-selling book, *I'm Having It.*

Listen to Kathy on *Imperfect Brilliance* on Mondays on A2Zen.fm

Connect or plan your own personal retreat: https://www.facebook.com/KathyWilliamsTransformationAgent/ and at www.iotransformation.com for fun videos & freebies.

Classes ~ Healing Sessions ~ Access Bars Trainings ~ Yoga Therapy

www.iotransformation.com

# Chapter 19

## Toolbox for Bullied Kids

By Petrina Fava

Every child knows with certainty that the sky is blue. Try telling a kid that the sky is green and they'll giggle at the absurdity of your suggestion. Imagine if they knew what an incredible gift they are to the world with that same unequivocal certainty. What would be different if kids knew that all judgments are lies and that separation is not real? What if kids could be so sure of their greatness that nothing could ever dull their shine; not even mean, vicious words or cruel acts of violence? It is possible.

### My Heart Hurts

One day during his first week of kindergarten, my five-year-old son said to me in a very fake, whiney voice: "Mommeeeee... my heaart hurrrts." "What do you mean?" I asked him. "Are you having chest pain? Do we need to go to the hospital?" I'm a nurse. This is the first place my mind goes. "No mommy," he said in his normal voice. "You know, when someone says something mean and then your heart gets hurt. Every time somebody says something mean it makes a black mark on your heart." I know he is repeating something someone has told him. A kind of rage builds inside me...*who would say such shit to a kid? A black mark on your heart? Don't they know kids take this stuff literally?!* "Oh. I see. Who told you that?" I question gently. "My teacher," he responds happily and then skips off to play with his legos. I soften. I know his teacher has tried to explain what happens when people are mean to each other, in a concrete way to a group of four and five year-olds; that mean words can cause feelings to be hurt and that sometimes it can have a lasting impact.

This conversation had me wondering a few things: Is there a moment when kids don't actually believe the mean words? Are they able to let some things go more easily than we think? Are they initially just aware that it feels yucky? What happens after that? When do they begin to label it and buy it as real? And when do they decide that it hurts? Is it possible that telling kids that we are sad and hurt when someone is mean to us begins to actually create that in their reality? What if the yucky feeling is not our hearts hurting, but just information— an awareness of something? And what if that something has nothing to do with us? If we didn't suggest that mean words caused us to be sad, would kids have a different choice?

## Separation and Judgment are Lies

Is it possible that the entire concept of bullying is a lie? What if putting a stop to bullies is not the answer? I hear some of you screaming.... *"WHAT is she talking about?! Kids and teens all over the world are suffering crippling depression, attempting suicide; many of them have succeeded....all because of horrible mean bullies!"* Yes. There are people in the world who are vicious and mean. This is simply a fact, there is no judgment here. People just choose that, even little kids. And yes, children all over the world are very much impacted by words, actions, sneers, ridicule and rudeness. What if they didn't have to be? What if we could show kids how to look at what a person is choosing and not be at the effect of it, no matter how horrible it is?

Bullying is deeply rooted in a right and wrong reality. This reality tells us that bullying is wrong. The bullies are wrong and should be shamed and the child being bullied is poor, helpless and should be protected. What would change if we stopped labelling everything as right or wrong and saw it all as interesting information? What if we started asking some questions? Asking questions opens the doors of possibility and allows you to choose based on awareness. Making judgments and drawing conclusions slam the doors of possibility shut. Conclusions only lead you to the option you have already decided are right. How much more clarity could we have to know what might be required to change this if we didn't have the blur of judgment in the way?

## Your Point of View Creates Your Reality

Your point of view creates your reality, your reality does not create your point of view. This one minute conversation with my son was such a gift. If your point of view creates your reality and your reality is, "words hurt me," what is that creating in your body? What other things are we teaching our children that inadvertently suggest they are less than and at the effect of the words, actions and unkindness of others? What conflictual reality are we creating for kids when we instruct them not to be mean to others because words hurt, but then advise them to ignore the unkindness that is directed at them?

The schoolyard gate is an interesting place to hear parents react to bullying. There is such a heavy cloud of judgment, fear, anger and a heroic need to protect and rescue their child. "Why are kids so mean?...What's wrong with that kid's parents? Don't they teach him anything?... My poor kid, he's so afraid to come to school... I'm going straight to the principal's office, that kid should be expelled!" I know the idea that children are weaker than adults is such a lie. In my 18 years as a pediatric nurse, I have watched kids get through some really intense changes in their bodies that most adults would balk at. And I've seen many of them do it with without giving up their joy or their laughter.

Kids are far greater than most of us will ever give them credit for and they know so much. Sometimes, in an attempt to validate the adults they love, kids begin to replace what they know intrinsically with the opinions of the adults around them. Children are extremely intuitive, easily picking up on all the subtle thoughts, feelings and emotions of others. What points of view, judgments and conclusions do we as adults project at our kids that have them believe they are victims? I headed to the Anti-cyber Bullying Statutes by John Hayward and Dictionary.com to investigate how we define bullying. I discovered these two very interesting explanations. As you read them, I invite you to be aware of the sensations in your body and to notice which words jump out for you:

"Bullying is defined as repeated intimidation, over time, of a physical, verbal and psychological nature of a less powerful person by a more powerful person or group of persons. It is repetitive and encompasses an intrinsic power imbalance between the bully and the person being bullied who generally is incapable of self-defense. It can be physical (e.g., punching), verbal (e.g. name-calling) and/or social (e.g., spreading rumors)."

"a blustering, quarrelsome, overbearing person who habitually badgers and intimidates smaller or weaker people."

Here is what stands out for me:

"...of a less powerful person by a more powerful person"

"...encompasses an intrinsic power imbalance"

"....incapable of self-defense"

"....badgers and intimidates smaller or weaker people"

What are we saying to our kids with our attempt to be the more knowledgeable adult; to protect and rescue? That they are victims, incapable of self-defense? That the bully is more powerful? Are we unintentionally giving children the message that they are weak while telling them that they're tough enough to get through it? How much do kids perceive the underlying victim energy being projected at them, regardless of our encouraging words? Let's truly empower our children with more than just words of encouragement. Let's give them the tools to recognize that the power is in their own hands.

## Allowance and Interesting Point of View

What if letting go of judgment and having allowance for people who choose to bully is the beginning of creating something completely different? I hear you yelling again. *"Letting go of judgment? Having allowance for bullies?! Is she crazy? It is NOT ok to let kids be vicious to other kids!!"* You are correct, it is absolutely not ok. Make no mistake; allowance is not tolerance or acceptance. It is not being a doormat or turning the other cheek. Allowance is the willingness to see everything as just an interesting point of view. It's the letting go of judgment in order to have clarity about what is actually going on. Only then can we have the awareness of what's truly required to change something. This kind of clarity is not possible with the clouds of judgment, anger and defense in the way. We can teach allowance to kids while also empowering them to be and do whatever is required to change any situation.

What does that look like in day to day life on the playground? It may be different for each child and for each situation, so being in the question is vital. A great question to start with is, "What's required for my child to be empowered? Will rescuing the child empower him? Or will it invalidate him?" I have often asked my own kids, "What do you know about this? What do you know about this kid? What's required?" Encouraging the child to ask himself, "What's required to change this?" is empowering and validates his knowing. What have you decided is inappropriate to teach your child to do or be? Do you have the point of view that it would be wrong to tell your child to shove the bully back? What if in some situations that is what's truly required to create something greater for everyone, even the bully? If you've decided that any kind of violence is wrong then you won't allow yourself to see where it can be a contribution. Awareness is the ability to see something for what it really is, not what you think it should be.

## Light and Heavy

The truth will make you feel light and a lie will make you feel heavy. There is no one truth, only what is true for YOU.

Let me give you a quick example:

"You are so stinking ugly. You're fat and stupid, too. What a worthless pile of shit you are. Everybody hates you, why don't you go kill yourself?" Notice your body. Light? Or heavy?

"I am so grateful that you are reading this chapter I've written. Thank you for receiving it, I truly hope that it creates a difference in your world." Is that light or heavy?

With this tool, when kids perceive the heaviness of the judgment being projected at them, they can identify it as a lie instead of buying it as true and allowing it to impact their body. Anything that's heavy is a lie. Period. It's a great tool for kids to use when choosing which friends they would like to be around, too. *"Does being with this person make me feel light, joyful, giddy, and warm? Or do I feel heavy, twisted and contracted when I am with them? It feels so heavy when I'm around kids who are gossiping, I wonder who else I could hang out with. What about that thing the teacher just told me; light or heavy? Is it true for me?"*

Do you remember thinking your parents and teachers were all-knowing and then years later crumbling at the sudden awareness that they actually weren't? I wonder what would change if kids didn't buy the lie that adults know more than they do, or that they are smarter because they are more experienced? Would there be fewer sexual assaults on children if we empowered them to use their awareness instead of teaching them that adults are always right? Would there be less frustration and struggle amongst teens if they were able to choose using their awareness of what's true for them? Would they have to resist anyone or anything if they were allowed to know what they know?

## Receiving Judgment

Imagine for a moment that every time you received a judgment, a one-hundred dollar bill appeared in each of your pockets. Would you be as upset as you usually are when someone judged you? Or would you get really excited and then go out and buy pants with lots of pockets in them, ready to receive more? I hear you loud and clear. *"First she tells me not to judge, now she's telling me to receive judgment. What's up with this?"* Receiving judgment is not the same as believing the judgment or taking it into your body. That's actually what happens when you resist judgment. Receiving judgment can be done by lowering your barriers and allowing yourself to be totally vulnerable as you let the judgment pass through your body.

As adults, we have learned to put up gigantic, impenetrable barriers to judgment and resist it furiously. Thankfully, most kids have not had quite as much experience with putting up barriers as adults have. Lowering your barriers can take some practice. I've discovered a fun way to play with receiving judgment. I've given each of my kids a "Judgment Jar" in which I contribute money each time they happily laugh at a judgment that has been projected at them. It has created more than I could have imagined. There are days my daughter runs through the front door after school yelling, "Mommy!!! Johnny called me stupid!! Can I have two dollars?!" It's hilarious and amazing.

## Do You Have My Back?

Empowering children does not mean leaving them to fend for themselves. I am not suggesting that intervening is wrong; in fact, it may sometimes be what is required. This is different from rescuing, though. As parents, we can help our kids get clear about which choice will create greater. The key here is not having a point of view about any of it. Having any point of view at all, even if it's one we consider to be right, helpful or well- meaning, becomes a barrier to awareness.

My pre-teen daughter came home one afternoon and told me someone was persistently being rude to her at school. She asked me to intervene by telling her friend to stop and calling her friend's mom. I encouraged her to ask questions about what was required for this to change. I told my daughter I knew she had the ability to handle this without me. For days she insisted I save her, and for days I insisted she had the capacity to change this herself. I had the point of view that I was not going to rescue her because I knew she could handle it. I was not asking questions. Finally, I asked myself, "What does she really desire from me? What's required here?" I realized that she needed to know I was always going to have her back. I was pushing my point of view of "you're strong enough to do this by yourself" onto her. I made a conclusion that calling the girl's mom was the wrong thing to do. I thought I was empowering her but I was not—because I wasn't listening. I wasn't acknowledging what was true for her or trusting her awareness of what was going to work. This conversation has been yet another enormous gift to me. How many conclusions did I have in the way that I thought were "good" ones? The thing about judgments and conclusions is that it doesn't matter whether we consider them to be good or bad; they are walls, smoke screens to true awareness. I gave her a hug. "I will always be here for you" I told her, "I will have your back no matter what." And while I still wasn't willing to rescue her, I began to see that she was so deep in her own beliefs that she just couldn't see any other way out besides me calling the girl's mom. I became a sounding board for her to ask some questions and tap into her own knowing so she could choose how to approach the situation in a way that would create the greatest outcome for her. I also called the girl's mom. When I did, I saw where this mom was functioning from drama and it gave me the information we needed to change the situation completely. What did my daughter know about calling this girl's mom that I didn't? When we are willing to receive them, the gifts of awareness our children give to us are incredible.

What if we're not here to teach our children anything? What if we're not here to mold them, set them up for a good life, or even help them be good people? What if we could receive the gift they are, exactly as they are, with absolutely no point of view about how or what they should be or do? What kind of future could be created by a generation of people who, as children, were acknowledged for everything they knew and whose gifts were fully received by those around them?

To each of my amazing children...thank you for being the catalyst I needed to take a long look at myself. Not to judge where I needed to be better for you, but to acknowledge my own magic and my own gifts; the ones that I myself have buried under years of trying to fit into this reality. I will continue to honor the gift that I am to the world and expand my life in ways I may not even be dreaming of yet. I know that as I do this, you may acknowledge the amazing gift you are to the world, too. As I lower my own barriers and go beyond the limitations of judgment and fear, the possibility for you to choose beyond barriers expands. Or, perhaps you won't choose that for yourself... and that's ok too, because I have your back no matter what you choose.

# About the Author

PETRINA FAVA

At some point in her adult life as she considered having children, Petrina Fava decided that being a mom was something she was not going to mess up. She had messed up a lot of things in her life, but she was determined that this was *not* going to be one of them. She was going to get this one *right*! Her husband was confident that she had endless patience and was sure she would be an excellent mom; it was one of the reasons he had married her in the first place. She wasn't exactly prepared for what was going to show up.

Petrina loved kids and became a pediatric nurse at the age of 21. She happily brought home her firstborn daughter and cared for her confidently, knowing she had the skills to take care of a baby. Many years of nursing critically ill children had provided her with all the training she required to feed, bathe, soothe and comfort her daughter. Sure, it was stressful at times, but Petrina handled it well. She and her husband added two more children to their lives, and as their family grew and the kids got older, Petrina was less and less able to micromanage their daily lives. She began to feel lost, unprepared and out of control. While she knew how to take care of her children's health, her training as a nurse had not taught her anything about tantrums over the wrong colored cup, spilled breakfast cereal, sibling rivalry, potty training and grocery shopping with three very loud kids in tow. She began to read books, meet with other moms, look for answers and judge herself immensely for failing at being a good mom. What was happening to her patience? Why was she shouting? Where were these horrible feelings of annoyance with her sweet children coming from? Why did she think they were manipulating her? Who was she turning into? Was her husband disappointed in her? Why did she just want to go to work seven days a week?

Her brother introduced her to the tools of Access Consciousness® in 2009. He taught her very first Bars® class and she has been playing with the tools of Access Consciousness and creating her life in all kinds of unexpected ways since then. The Access tools have empowered Petrina to increase her awareness, acknowledge her capacities, drop the self-judgment and step into her potency to create greater.

When Petrina found the tools of Access Consciousness, she was intrigued by it's very unique and almost controversial perspective on parenting. Of course, she loved it. She played with questions like, "What if nothing you've ever done has been wrong?" and "Would you be willing to be a horrible mother?... What would create the most ease for all of us?" Thankfully, Petrina has given up trying to be a "good mom" and just keeps choosing something different every day. She *knows* that kids are incredibly aware and much smarter than most people ever give them credit for.

When Petrina Fava started working as an RN with critically ill children and their families at Toronto's SickKids hospital

18 years ago, she began to notice that kids had an astonishing capacity to move past drama, and embrace laughter and joy no matter what was happening with their bodies. For years she has watched kids endure painful procedures and then proceed to laugh, smile and play the second it was over as if nothing ever happened. No judgment, no significance; just the next choice. It's magical and inspiring. She is excited to share the tools of Access with kids of all ages all over the world and empower them to create their own lives.

Petrina began to explore other ways to work with children and in 2008, she learned to teach Infant Massage and started her own business, Gentle Connections. She expanded her classes to include Kids Yoga and *GROOVE* Dance. Most recently, she began teaching Nursing at George Brown College in Toronto and enjoys showing students how to be in the question rather than use judgments and conclusions when caring for others.

Petrina is an Access Bars & Body Process Facilitator as well as a Right Body for You™ Intro Facilitator. She has used the Access tools to create her business in interesting ways. She is the host of her own radio show called *Messy Adventures in Living* on A2zen.fm, and is a best-selling author in the Amazon #1 Best Selling collaboration book, *Creations: Conscious Conception and Fertility, Pregnancy and Birth.*

Petrina is so grateful for her three bright, spirited children who keep showing her all the places she is holding onto judgment and fear, and who provide her plenty of opportunities to let that all go and replace it with laughter. They have been a gift beyond anything she could have ever imagined or planned. Every day is a messy adventure!

You are invited to connect with Petrina at any of the following:

www.petrinafava.com

www.facebook.com/petrinafavachoosinghappy
www.petrina.fava@accessconsciousness.com
http://a2zen.fm/podcast/messy-adventures-in-living-petrina-fava/

CPSIA information can be obtained
at www.ICGtesting.com
Printed in the USA
LVOW04s0835270116
471782LV00011B/72/P